In the Kitchen with the

CHIPPENDALES ®

In the Kitchen with the
CHIPPENDALES®

More Than 70 Romantic Recipes to Tempt, Tease, and Tantalize

by Stacy Rae Rubalcaba

COURAGE BOOKS

AN IMPRINT OF RUNNING PRESS
PHILADELPHIA • LONDON

Exclusive Licensing Agency
Hakan & Associates, Inc.
10800 Farley, Suite 310
Overland Park, KS 66210
ph:913-327-7900

© 1999

Chippendales®
7380 Sand Lake Road, Suite 350
Orlando, Fl 32819

Library of Congress Cataloging-in-Publication Number 98-68515
ISBN 0-7624-0569-4

Interior and cover design by Frances J. Soo Ping Chow
Edited by Gena M. Pearson and Caroline E. Tiger
Typography: ITC Berkeley and Poppl Residenz

This book may be ordered by mail from the publisher.
But try your bookstore first!

Published by Courage Books, an imprint of
Running Press Book Publishers
125 South Twenty-second Street
Philadelphia, Pennsylvania 19103-4399

Visit us on the web!
www.runningpress.com
www.chippendales.com

Table of Contents

Passionate Prelude 9

Appeteasers 15

Lettuce Love 33

On the Side 43

Don't Stop Now 55

Lubrications 75

Sweet Seductions 87

The Morning After 107

Menus to Make You Moan 117

Index 122

For Our International Audience 126

About the Chippendales® 128

Acknowledgments

First and foremost, I wish to thank the Chippendales® for having enough faith in me to make my fantasy into a reality, proving that dreams really can come true. My publisher did not laugh at me when I told him that I was born to write this book. He said great minds think alike when it comes to the feasibility of the food-and-sex concept, and then secured me for this daring project.

My editor was beyond wonderful, and her kindness and patience helped me every step of the way. I am positive that her arduous duty of critiquing my sexual scenarios and examining erotic pictures of seminaked men was a trying process, but she somehow managed to forge through it with stellar professionalism.

I will forever be grateful to all my girlfriends who generously shared their amorous ideas, helping me to expand my horizons. They were eager and willing students of mine in the art of seducing men through food. They passed my erotic eating classes with flying colors, proving that my theories really do work! I pay particular tribute to the women of the "M" Club.

I give a very special thanks to my colleagues and customers at the barber shop. The casual and relaxed atmosphere of the shop gave new meaning to the phrase, "let your hair down." Through this environment, the unique male psyche was revealed to me, enabling me to learn what makes men tick. On a personal note, the men in my life were an endless source of inspiration.

From the standpoint of my family, I wish to say thank you to my uncle, whom I love very much. His support and encouragement to better myself with education gave me the skills and confidence to succeed. My lovely mother schooled me in the art of social graces, love of beauty, and creative cooking. Finally, I thank my father. He gave me my greatest gifts of all. Without my lust for life and passion for love, there would be no motivation for this book or anything else. I love and miss my dad, my best friend.

Passionate Prelude

Nothing says romance more than an evening that begins with fine wine, leads to a fancy dinner, and ends with a decadent dessert. That's why my food fantasy dream date with a Chippendales® boy toy puts me in the mood quicker than anything.

Mr. Gorgeous arrives at my house for dinner carrying a dozen long-stemmed red roses, a bottle of French Champagne, and a small black satchel. His naughty smile begs me to ask what's in his bag of tricks. Special after-dinner secrets just for me, he says. Hmmm.

In the kitchen he pops my cork, and I prepare for our French Kiss, Champagne Cocktail that is. Mr. Sugar Pie mysteriously disappears for a few minutes. My excited mind wanders, wondering what this sexy man has up his sleeve. When he returns, we indulge in the bubbly, and the fun and dinner begin.

Knowing the aphrodisiac effect oysters have on men, I eagerly offer to hand-feed them to my hunk. As he reciprocates by feeding me, I mesmerize him by kissing the oysters with my sexy, pouty lips before I swallow them.

Stud Puppy's appreciative moans thank me for the gourmet salad that he savors, laced with raspberries, blueberries, blue cheese, and pecans. His eyes open wide as I serve him Juicy Tails—lobster that is. They're beautifully accompanied with long delicate asparagus spears and melted butter.

Honey Bun removes all the silverware, then informs me we will eat with our fingers. He surprises and pleases me with this food foreplay. The temperature rises as I gaze at him placing lobster meat in his eager mouth. He likes seeing me lock my lips around the long asparagus spears while the melted butter trickles slowly down my chin.

I have made luscious raspberry lip-shaped tarts for dessert, but he pours us some more Champagne instead. The intoxicating feeling makes me want more of everything. He takes me to the living room to dance cheek to cheek in front of the romantic crackling fire. Then he leads to me to my bedroom and tells me he's taking me to paradise. I gaze upon my bed, now completely adorned with rose petals. The flickering candlelight shows an assortment of edible body paints, chocolate syrup, and whipped cream. I never knew how artistic he was!

I can't find the words to describe the rest of this fantasy date, but it's safe to say I did visit paradise, and it's just this side of heaven. I've experienced the mysterious food-and-sex connection, and it was a night to remember. I wonder what my Chippendale® wants for dinner tomorrow night?

Women are fortunate to have the Chippendale® men. If it weren't for this phenomenon, who would we have to excite and stimulate us in such a sexy way? Society caters constantly to men by providing books, videos, live shows, etc., but we always get the short end of the stick. I think it's time for a change. Women are visually oriented too, but our outlets are limited. This is why the sensuous Chippendales® men provide such a valuable service, and why we love them so much.

Recently, I attended a Chippendales® performance with my three girlfriends—a hair-stylist, a graphic designer, and an attorney. Their performance inspired me to create two outrageous dishes, Chick on a Bed of Roses (Chicken and Rose Petal Mole) and Between the Sheets (Pasta and Polenta Beds with Red Pepper Sauce). During the show, one stud muffin did all these incredible things with a long-stemmed red rose. He started to . . . well, you just had to be there. And another very sexy man did a horizontal dance on a bed between two satin sheets. That's how I got a visual picture of these two tasty dishes. I highly recommend you see their show when it comes to your city. They might inspire you, too.

In the Kitchen with the Chippendales® is a lighthearted and fun way to put your man in the mood with food. Mouthwatering photos of the Chippendales® are especially designed to stimulate your appetites. Everything comes together with the help of Menus to Make You Moan, listed at the very end of the book. These provide ideas for combining the recipes inside to create ten different feasts, each sizzlingly seductive in its very own way.

Don't be surprised if your man looks toward you with hungry eyes after he has devoured these seductive spreads with gusto. After all, the way to a man's heart is through his stomach; I just show you a different route.

Before you get to the recipes, here are a few features to further enhance your sensual gastronomic pleasures.

Sexual Savvies

If a recipe contains an aphrodisiac, an arousing scent, or the potential for an erotic eating method, a Sexual Savvy symbol will alert you to the steamy stimuli. Consult the key below and proceed with caution when you discover one of these stirring symbols.

Key to Symbols

This recipe contains one or more aphrodisiacs.

When preparing and serving this recipe, don't be surprised if your man perks up at its arousing scent.

This food can and should be eaten erotically. Use your imagination.

Sensual Scenarios

Another unique aspect is Sensual Scenarios—at the end of some recipes, you'll find these seductive food fantasy adventures to explore with your lover. These are just starting points—feel free to expand and elaborate on these fantasies as you grow inspired. Sensual Scenarios are peppered throughout the book to add more variety and spice to your experience.

Erotic Eating

The art of eating can be a delicious form of seduction. Forget everything your mother taught you about good table manners. Playing with your food is fun, but make it look good.

Slowly and sensuously lick or bite a piece of food, and your man will experience how provocative and primal your new way of communicating can be. He might be so intrigued that you could teach him a thing or two. The whole idea is to stir things up and to use body language that titillates. But remember, if you tease, you must please.

When you luxuriate in this type of sensuous prelude, everything must be done slowly, deliberately, and with eye contact. Now that you have mastered the art of erotic eating, read on to learn which foods can be eaten in an erotic manner.

As a general rule of thumb, most foods can be eaten with fingers. But bite-size ones are good erotic food candidates. Many fruits are perfect because they come in natural bite-size packages. Try any berry—strawberries, raspberries, and blackberries. Don't forget cherries. They come with their own handle so you can dangle them over your lover's lips. Or you can pluck grapes off the vine, one by one, hand-feeding them to your lover. Any fruit like melons, apples, peaches, pears, or orange segments can be cut into bite-size pieces and are very suitable as well as delicious. And bananas are one of the all-time best erotic foods. They're so versatile. I'll just leave it at that!

Last but not least are sweets. Pudding, mousse, honey, ice cream cones, popsicles, and suckers are foods that will pleasure both you and your lover, so indulge.

That about takes care of my food selections, but I am sure there are lots more, so experiment and see what you can come up with. There are no right or wrong ways to eat like a sex kitten. Do whatever makes you purr.

Arousing Edibles

bananas, caviar, Champagne, chili peppers, chocolate, coffee, cucumbers, edible flowers (roses, pansies, lavender, nasturtiums), hot mustard, lobster, mussels, onions, oysters, saffron, Wasabi (Japanese horseradish)

Aphrodisiac Foods

Aphrodisiacs are believed to have magical powers that excite sexual desire. But regardless of the countless claims a food has in the libido department, if you are receptive to the idea of it having those properties and want to believe that it's true, it will be. So with that thought, keep an open mind.

Arousing Scents

For women: licorice, cucumber, and baby talc powder
For men: pumpkin pie, baked sweets like cinnamon buns, lavender, strawberries, and vanilla

Scents for Your Senses

You always knew the smell of baked goods coming from your kitchen attracted your man, but did you also know that it produces strong below-the-belt responses? Think about it the next time you bake your sweetie a pumpkin pie or cinnamon buns.

Now, because these racy recipes are teamed with yummy Chippendales® men, I will understand if this is your motivation for purchasing this book. But please, don't drool on the pictures! At least try some of these sumptuous recipes.

Appeteasers

Appetizers

Oysters Rock-Yer-Fella 18

Spring Roll in the Hay 19

Topless Tapas 21

Adam and Edam in the Garden of Eatin' 22

Baby Cakes 23

Put Out the Fire Man! 24

Gotcha Focaccia 25

Harem Hummus 26

Honeymoon Salmon Tartare 27

Be Still My Beating Heart Dip 28

Gigolo Shrimp Cocktail 28

Honeydew This, Honeydew That 30

Go Man-Go Salsa 31

Oysters Rock-Yer-Fella

Oysters Rockefeller *Serves 4*

12 oysters	Salt
Rock salt	Cayenne
2 teaspoons salted butter	½ cup thawed chopped frozen spinach, patted dry
1 tablespoon finely chopped yellow onion	¼ cup fresh bread crumbs
1 clove garlic, finely chopped	¼ cup grated Parmesan cheese
	Paprika, for garnish
1 tablespoon finely chopped fresh parsley	Yogurt-coated raisin, for garnish

1. Preheat the oven to 450°F.

2. Open the oysters and discard the top shells. Remove the oysters from the bottom shells and pat dry with paper towels. Return the oysters to the bottom shells.

3. Fill an 18 x 12-inch baking pan with rock salt. Place the oysters on top of the rock salt.

4. In a small skillet set over low heat, melt the butter. Add the onion and garlic and sauté for 1 minute, or until the onion and garlic are soft. Remove the skillet from the heat and stir in the parsley. Season to taste with salt and cayenne.

5. Spread each oyster with the onion and parsley mixture. Top with the spinach, bread crumbs, Parmesan cheese, and paprika.

6. Bake for 9 to 10 minutes, or until the crumbs are browned.

Serving Suggestion: Place the yogurt-covered raisin on top of one of the oysters to simulate a pearl.

Sensual Scenario: Your lover is a sexy pirate and you are his wench. You're in a very adventurous and playful mood. You can almost smell the salt air and feel the ocean breeze. You look every bit the wench wearing your sexy off-the-shoulder peasant dress complete with bosom-enhancing lace-up corset. It practically offers you up to him. Of course, he likes what he sees. It's time to serve your pirate his tasty oysters. You inform him that whoever discovers the "pearl" gets their sexual wish for the night. The rest of the night it's Oysters Rock-Yer-Fella while you shiver his timber.

Spring Roll in the Hay
Spring Roll on a Bed of Fried Rice Noodles *Serves 6*

Vegetable oil	2 tablespoons water
2 eggs	1 teaspoon finely chopped fresh ginger
¼ pound pork tenderloin, cut into about ¼-inch pieces	1 teaspoon finely chopped garlic
½ cup shredded cabbage	1 tablespoon sweet-and-sour sauce
½ cup (2 ounces) bean sprouts	1 teaspoon soy sauce
⅓ cup finely chopped mushrooms	1 teaspoon cornstarch blended with 2 teaspoons water
¼ cup chopped white onion	White pepper
¼ cup finely chopped green onions	6 spring roll wrappers
1 small carrot cut into julienne strips	Rice noodles, for garnish

1. Heat ½ teaspoon oil in a wok or large nonstick skillet set over medium heat. Beat 1 egg in a small bowl. Add to the skillet and scramble for about 1 minute, or until firm. Set aside.

2. In the same pan, heat 1 tablespoon oil over high heat. Add the pork and stir-fry for about 2 minutes, or until no longer pink.

3. Add the cabbage, bean sprouts, mushrooms, white and green onions, carrot, ginger, and garlic. Stir-fry for about 2 minutes, or until crisp-tender.

4. Combine the 2 tablespoons water, sweet-and-sour sauce, soy sauce, and cornstarch mixture in a small bowl. Season to taste with white pepper. Add to the vegetables and stir until the sauce thickens. Remove from the heat and stir in the scrambled egg. Set aside for a few minutes to cool.

5. For each spring roll, lay a spring roll wrapper flat on a work surface. Keep the remaining wrappers covered to prevent drying. Place 2 heaping tablespoons of the vegetable mixture in the center of the wrapper. Fold a bottom corner over filling, and then fold over left and right corners. Gently roll over once to completely enclose the filling. Beat the remaining egg. Brush the top corner of the wrapper with the egg. Fold over and press to seal. Keep covered with a damp towel while assembling the remaining spring rolls.

6. Fill a wok or deep heavy-bottomed, medium-sized saucepan with 2 to 3 inches of oil. Heat the oil over medium heat until it reaches 360°F.

7. Carefully add the spring rolls, a few at a time, to the hot oil. Fry for 2 to 3 minutes, or until golden brown, carefully turning occasionally. Drain on paper towels.

8. Add the rice noodles to the oil and fry for 1 to 2 seconds or until triple in size. Remove immediately and drain on paper towels.

Serving Suggestions : Serve with sweet-and-sour sauce and hot mustard for dipping. For a fun presentation, scatter the fried rice noodles on a large serving plate and top with the spring rolls. Place small individual dipping-sauce bowls on the side of each serving plate.

Sensual Scenario: Spring has just sprung. You and your lover are having a romantic picnic beside a pond. Your mood is adventurous and frisky, and your lover likes this side of you. You look so cute in your romantic coun-try skirt and white blouse. After you hand-feed him the delicious spring roll, you watch his eyes light up when you ask him for a real Spring Roll in the Hay.

Topless Tapas

Ham and Potato Croquettes *Serves 4*

2 tablespoons olive oil	4 drops hot pepper sauce
2 tablespoons finely chopped yellow onion	1 tablespoon finely chopped fresh parsley
2 cloves garlic, finely chopped	2 teaspoons finely chopped cilantro
2 teaspoons finely chopped red bell pepper	Salt
	Freshly cracked black pepper
¾ cup (4 ounces) finely chopped ham	Flour, for dredging
1 tablespoon all-purpose flour	2 eggs, beaten
3 large potatoes, boiled, peeled, and quartered	Dry, fine bread crumbs, for dredging
⅓ cup whole milk	Vegetable oil, for frying

1. Heat the olive oil in a medium skillet set over medium heat. Add the onion, garlic, bell pepper, and ham and cook for about 1 minute, or until the onion begins to soften. Remove from the heat and set aside.

2. In a small bowl, combine the milk and flour with a fork until smooth. In a large glass or plastic bowl, mash the potatoes by hand with a potato masher until smooth. Add the milk mixture, onion mixture, pepper sauce, parsley, and cilantro to the potatoes, and blend well. Add salt and pepper to taste. Cover and refrigerate for 2 to 3 hours, or until chilled and mixture is firm.

3. Form the potato mixture into 2-inch cone-shaped croquettes. Dredge in flour, then dip into the beaten eggs and roll in bread crumbs. Refrigerate croquettes for another 30 minutes.

4. Fill a deep, heavy-bottomed, medium-sized saucepan with 4 inches of vegetable oil. Heat the oil over medium heat until it reaches 365°F. Fry the croquettes in the hot oil making sure they are completely submerged. Fry for 2 to 3 minutes, turning once, until golden brown. Drain on paper towels.

Serving Suggestion: Place these beautiful and tasty tapas on a large plate, pointy end up. For a beautiful visual as well as delicious accompaniment, try serving this with either Go Man-Go Salsa or Put Out the Fire Man! Spicy Salsa (see page 31 and page 24).

Sensual Scenario: You are a topless waitress serving your lover in a flamenco bar. The lighting is dim, and the musky scent of warm bodies fills the air. Your lover's heart starts to pound to the beat of the strumming of Spanish guitars. Suddenly, he grabs you for a seductive dance. You are shocked, but love it. The red rose that adorns your hair falls to the ground when he very powerfully twirls and dips you. The two of you spend the rest of the evening doing the horizontal flamenco.

Adam and Edam in the Garden of Eatin'
Edam Cheese with Apple Wedges for Dipping *Serves 2*

One 5-to-6-inch round Edam or Gouda cheese, at room temperature	Nutmeg, for garnish
2 to 4 tablespoons heavy cream	Apple wedges and assorted crackers, for serving

1. Cut a 4- to 5-inch diameter heart pattern from a piece of heavy paper. Pin the heart pattern on top of the cheese round. With a small paring knife, cut around the paper heart, making sure to cut all the way through the red rind. With a small spoon, carefully remove the cheese heart and set aside. Hollow out the cheese round, leaving a ¼-inch shell.

2. In a food processor or with an electric mixer, combine 2 tablespoons of the cream with the cheese removed from the round, beating until the consistency of a paste and adding more cream as needed.

3. Mound the whipped cheese mixture into the cheese shell. Garnish with dash of nutmeg. Keep chilled until ready to serve. Serve with apple wedges and crackers.

Serving Suggestions: Use a variety of apples for a more colorful presentation, alternating them in a circle around the Edam cheese. Arrange the crackers in a circle around the apple wedges. A group of apples on your table are an appropriate centerpiece.

Sensual Scenario: Life is good in the Garden of Eden with Adam. You feel wonderful about your body and hair. In fact, you don't even care if your fig leaf falls. You are a temptress. The bold attitude you have is perfect, because you plan on committing the original sin. Adam senses your confidence, and likes what he sees. The time is right for tempting Adam. You know what to do, Eve.

Baby Cakes
Crab Cakes with Lemon Mustard Sauce *Serves 2*

Crab Cakes	2 tablespoons vegetable oil
1 pound lump crabmeat, picked over	
	Lemon Mustard Sauce
¼ cup finely chopped red bell pepper	¾ cup mayonnaise
¼ cup finely chopped green bell pepper	¼ cup sour cream
¼ cup finely chopped yellow onion	1 tablespoon Dijon mustard
¼ cup finely chopped celery	¼ teaspoon grated lemon zest
2 tablespoons finely chopped fresh parsley	¼ teaspoon lemon pepper
	¼ teaspoon cracked black pepper
2 eggs, beaten	1 teaspoon honey
¾ cup dry bread crumbs	1 teaspoon lemon juice
¾ teaspoon salt	Salt
1 teaspoon lime juice	Lemon and lime wedges, for garnish
1 dash hot pepper sauce	

1. Prepare the crab cakes: In a large bowl, combine the crab, red and green bell peppers, onion, celery, parsley, eggs, bread crumbs, salt, lime juice, and hot pepper sauce. Mix gently to avoid breaking up lumps of crabmeat.

2. Divide the crab mixture into 6 equal portions and shape into patties.

3. Heat the oil in a large sauté pan set over medium heat. Carefully place the crab cakes in the pan and cook 2 to 3 minutes on each side, or until golden brown. Remove from the pan and drain on paper towels. Keep warm.

4. Prepare the lemon mustard sauce: In a small bowl, blend the mayonnaise, sour cream, Dijon mustard, lemon zest, lemon pepper, black pepper, honey, lemon juice, and salt to taste.

Serving Suggestions: Serve the crab cakes on lettuce leaves topped with lemon mustard sauce and garnish with lemon and lime wedges. This sumptuous treat will show your Baby Cakes how much he is appreciated.

Put Out the Fire Man!

Spicy Fresh Salsa *Serves 4*

2 large tomatoes, finely chopped	2 tablespoons finely chopped cilantro
1 tablespoon finely chopped yellow onion	1 tablespoon lime juice
	1 tablespoon olive oil
1 tablespoon finely chopped green onion	1 clove garlic, finely chopped
	Salt
2 to 3 pickled jalapeño peppers, finely chopped	Cayenne

1. Combine the tomatoes, yellow and green onions, jalapeño peppers, cilantro, lime juice, oil, and garlic in a medium bowl and toss gently. Season to taste with salt and cayenne.

2. Cover and chill for at least 30 minutes.

Serving Suggestion: Serve with corn or flour tortilla chips. Use this salsa on all meats, eggs, tacos, burritos, and anything else you can think of for a quick way to ignite the evening.

Sensual Scenario: The more salsa you eat, the hotter you both become. Tell your Fire Man, if he can put out your fire, you'll reward him with an ice-cold Mexican beer. Keep a bucket of ice handy. A cube slowly dragged on hot skin has a nice cooling effect as it melts, and it gives you goosebumps. Hot, lively, and spicy describe your attitude since you've been dancing to the sensuous rhythms of salsa music. As your Fire Man twirls you, your secret is revealed underneath your red dancing dress. No panties! Well, you're on fire, what does he expect?

Gotcha Focaccia

Pesto, Chicken, and Tomato Pizza *Serves 2*

¼ cup purchased pesto

One 12-inch purchased focaccia shell

½ cup shredded mozzarella cheese

¼ cup grated Parmesan cheese

1 cup chopped cooked chicken

1 ripe tomato, sliced

½ cup pitted black olives, halved

¼ cup thinly sliced yellow bell pepper

2 tablespoons finely chopped red onion

Salt

Freshly cracked black pepper

1. Preheat the oven to 450°F.

2. Spread the pesto evenly over the focaccia. Sprinkle with the mozzarella and Parmesan cheeses. Evenly arrange the chicken, tomato, olives, and bell pepper over the cheeses. Sprinkle with the onion and season to taste with salt and pepper.

3. Place on a baking sheet. Bake for 3 to 5 minutes, or until the cheeses melt. Cut into pie-shaped wedges and serve immediately.

Harem Hummus

Hummus Dip *Serves 2*

One 16-ounce can garbanzo beans, drained

2 cloves garlic, finely chopped

1½ tablespoons lemon juice

1 tablespoon tamari (see Note)

1 tablespoon tahini (sesame paste) (see Note)

3 teaspoons finely chopped fresh parsley

2 tablespoons olive oil

Freshly cracked black pepper

Whole pitted black olives, for garnish

2 pitas, quartered, for serving

Olive oil, for brushing pita bread

1. Preheat the oven to 500°F.

2. In a food processor, mix the garbanzo beans, garlic, lemon juice, tamari, tahini, 2 teaspoons of the parsley, and 2 tablespoons oil until smooth. Season to taste with pepper. Pour into a small serving bowl. Garnish with the remaining 1 teaspoon parsley and olives.

3. Brush oil on 1 side of the quartered pita breads, and place on a baking sheet. Bake 2 to 3 minutes, or until light golden brown. Serve pita bread with hummus for dipping.

Note: Tamari is a dark Japanese soy sauce available at Asian markets. Tahini can be purchased at natural foods stores.

Sensual Scenario: Tonight you are the star belly dancer in your sultan's harem. The erotic sounds of Middle Eastern belly-dancing music fills the air along with the earthy aroma of burning incense. Your provocative belly-dancing costume shows your bare midriff. Your sultan is obviously excited while you are doing the Dance of the Veils. When you think he wants you to come closer, offer to feed him the hummus dip instead. He'll be pleased that you're attending to his needs. After he is fed and full, resume your dance. This is your time to tease then please. 🌹

Honeymoon Salmon Tartare

Salmon Tartare *Serves 4*

½ pound smoked salmon, cut into ¼-inch pieces	1 cup sour cream
2 tablespoons finely chopped fresh chives	⅓ cup (3 ounces) golden osetra caviar
1 tablespoon finely chopped fresh dill	½ cup finely chopped red onion
1 tablespoon olive oil	½ cup capers
1 teaspoon rice wine vinegar	Fresh brown bread slices, about 3-inch square, for serving
Freshly cracked black pepper	Fresh purple chive flowers, for garnish
4 hard-cooked eggs, finely chopped	Lemon wedges, for garnish
	Dill sprigs, for garnish

1. In a medium bowl, combine the salmon, chives, dill, oil, rice wine vinegar, and pepper to taste. Mix well.

2. Mound one fourth of the salmon tartare in the centers of 4 dinner-sized plates. Mound the eggs, sour cream, caviar, onion, and capers around the salmon tartare. Arrange the bread around the edges of the plates.

3. To garnish, place the lemon wedges next to the salmon mounds. Arrange the chive flowers in the centers of the salmon. Place the dill sprigs on top of the sour cream.

Serving Suggestion: French Kiss Champagne Cocktail (see page 82) complements this dish quite well. Be sure to include small spoons or spreading knives with each plate. Even if you haven't yet had a honeymoon, you've probably experienced the "honeymoon stage." This is the very beginning of a relationship—when everything is new and exciting, and the two of you just can't get enough of each other. Try to recapture those romantic feelings when you serve this honeymoon-themed dish.

Be Still My Beating Heart Dip

Hot Artichoke Dip *Serves 4*

Two 16-ounce cans artichoke hearts, drained	Fresh steamed artichoke leaves, for garnish
1 cup mayonnaise	
1 cup grated Parmesan cheese	Assorted crackers and bread slices, for serving

1. Preheat the oven to 450°F.

2. In a medium bowl, mash the artichoke hearts well with clean hands, making sure to enjoy the sensation of the artichokes as they squish between your fingers. This is an exercise in sensation awareness. Start to enjoy the small pleasures in life. Add the mayonnaise and Parmesan cheese and mix well.

3. Spread the artichoke mixture in a 9-inch glass pie plate. Bake for 5 to 10 minutes, or until light golden brown.

Serving Suggestions : Arrange the artichoke leaves around the edge of the pie plate to hide the rim, overlapping them slightly. Serve the crackers and bread in a basket.

Gigolo Shrimp Cocktail

Bacon-wrapped Shrimp with Jalapeño Jelly Dipping Sauce
and Creamy Mustard Dipping Sauce *Serves 4*

16 large shrimp (1 pound), peeled leaving tails intact, and deveined	¾ cup jalapeño jelly (see Note)
¼ cup prepared horseradish	3 tablespoons honey mustard
	3 tablespoons mayonnaise
One 8-ounce can sliced water chestnuts, drained	½ teaspoon lemon juice
8 slices bacon	Salt
Vegetable oil, for frying	Chopped parsley, for garnish

1. Butterfly the shrimp and gently pat dry with paper towels. Fan the tails. Spread some of the horseradish inside each shrimp and insert 1 water chestnut slice. Cut each bacon slice into thirds. Wrap a bacon piece around each shrimp and secure with a wooden toothpick.

2. Fill a deep, heavy-bottomed, medium-sized saucepan with 2 to 3 inches of oil. Heat the oil over medium heat until it reaches 360°F. Fry the shrimp for 1 to 3 minutes, or until the bacon is crisp. Drain on paper towels. Use an oven mitt or long-handled slotted spoon when removing the shrimp to avoid hot splattering oil. Remove the toothpicks and keep warm.

3. In a small saucepan set over low heat, warm the jalapeño jelly for 2 to 3 minutes, stirring until completely melted. Set aside.

4. In a small saucepan, blend the mustard, mayonnaise, lemon juice, and salt to taste. Heat over low heat for 1 to 2 minutes, or until warm.

Note: Jalapeño jelly can be purchased at Mexican specialty markets.

Serving Suggestion: Spread the Jalapeño Jelly Dipping Sauce and Creamy Mustard Dipping Sauce on two separate large serving plates. Arrange half of the shrimp on each plate, making sure the shrimp tails are upright. Garnish with chopped parsley.

Sensual Scenario: Tonight your man is a gigolo. So have lots of money to buy him for a night of pleasure. The lights are dim, and sultry saxophone music plays in the background. You whet your gigolo's appetite by wearing a formfitting low-cut dress, sexy lingerie, and very high heels to show off your legs. You look hot and you know it. You can't wait to take control, but first one last piece of business. He sets the price, and you set the pace. I hope he can keep up with you.

Honeydew This, Honeydew That

Honeydew, Cucumber, and Kiwi Salsa *Serves 4*

¼ honeydew melon, peeled, seeded, and finely chopped

½ large cucumber, peeled, seeded, and finely chopped

2 kiwis, peeled and finely chopped

2 tablespoons finely chopped red onion

2 tablespoons finely chopped green onions

1 to 2 jalapeño or serrano peppers, seeded and finely chopped

2 tablespoons finely chopped cilantro

1 tablespoon lime juice

½ teaspoon granulated sugar

Green jalapeño jelly (see Note)

Salt

1. Combine the honeydew, cucumber, kiwi, red onions, green onion, jalapeño pepper, cilantro, lime juice, and sugar in a medium bowl and gently toss. Season to taste with jalapeño jelly and salt.

2. Cover and refrigerate until ready to serve.

Note: Jalapeño jelly can be purchased at Mexican specialty markets.

Serving Suggestion: Serve as an appetizer with corn or flour tortilla chips. Also an excellent topping for fish, chicken, or turkey. Try it on tacos and quesadillas, too.

Go Man-Go Salsa

Mango Peach Salsa *Serves 2*

1 mango, peeled, pitted, and finely chopped	1 tablespoon orange juice
2 peaches, peeled, seeded, and finely chopped	2 teaspoons olive oil
	1 teaspoon rice wine vinegar
2 tablespoons finely chopped red bell pepper	1 tablespoon light brown sugar
¼ cup finely chopped red onion	2 tablespoons finely chopped cilantro
1 jalapeño or serrano pepper, seeded and finely chopped	Red jalapeño jelly (see Note)
1 clove garlic, finely chopped	Salt
2 tablespoons lime juice	Cayenne

1. Combine the mango, peaches, bell pepper, red onion, jalapeño pepper, garlic, lime juice, orange juice, olive oil, rice wine vinegar, brown sugar, and cilantro in a medium bowl and gently toss. Season to taste with jalapeño jelly, salt, and cayenne.

2. Cover and refrigerate until ready to serve.

Note: Jalapeño jelly can be purchased at Mexican specialty markets.

Serving Suggestion: Serve as an appetizer with corn or flour tortilla chips. It is also an excellent topping for fish, chicken, turkey, beef, or pork. This unusual salsa makes a one-of-a-kind quesadilla or taco.

Lettuce
Love

Salads

Seize Her Caesar 36

Don't Be Blue, "I Love You" Salad 36

Sweet Pea Salad 37

South of Her Border if You Think

You Can Afford Her 38

Cucumber Heaven 39

Waves of Pleasure 40

Seize Her Caesar

Caesar Salad *Serves 4*

Two small heads romaine lettuce, washed and torn into pieces

3 cloves garlic, finely chopped

1 tablespoon anchovy paste

2 tablespoons olive oil

2 egg yolks, beaten (see Note)

3 tablespoons lemon juice

½ teaspoon freshly cracked black pepper

½ cup grated Parmesan cheese

1½ cups large croutons

1. Wrap lettuce in a damp cloth and refrigerate for at least ½ hour or until very crisp.

2. In a wooden salad bowl, whisk the garlic, anchovy paste, oil, egg yolks, lemon juice, and pepper until well blended.

3. Add the lettuce and Parmesan cheese, tossing until well coated. Top with the croutons and toss again. Serve immediately.

Serving Suggestion: This dish can be served as a main course topped with grilled chicken. Serve with crusty Italian or French bread.

Note: Because of the slight risk of salmonella, raw eggs should not be served to the very young, the ill or elderly, or to pregnant women.

Don't Be Blue, "I Love You" Salad

Blueberry, Blue Cheese, and Pecan Salad with Raspberry Dressing *Serves 4*

Salad

2 small heads of bibb or Boston lettuce, washed and torn into pieces

2 tablespoons salted butter

1 cup pecan halves

½ cup (4 ounces) crumbled blue cheese

1 cup blueberries

Raspberry Dressing	⅓ cup honey
¼ cup raspberry vinegar	
	½ cup olive oil
⅓ cup raspberries (may use frozen)	

1. Prepare the salad: Arrange the lettuce on 4 salad plates.

2. In a small skillet, set over medium heat, melt the butter (do not let it burn). Add the pecans and stir to coat well with the butter. Cook for 1 to 3 minutes, or until lightly browned, stirring occasionally. Arrange on top of the lettuce salad.

3. Sprinkle with the blue cheese. Arrange the blueberries on top.

4. Prepare the raspberry salad dressing: In a blender, mix the raspberry vinegar, raspberries, and honey. Blend on high for about 1 minute, or until smooth. Reduce the speed to medium. Slowly add the oil while blending. The dressing will become thickened and creamy.

5. Drizzle the dressing over the salads and serve immediately.

Sweet Pea Salad

Watercress, Mandarin Orange, and Cashew Salad *Serves 4*

Salad	3 tablespoons orange juice
2 bunches watercress, washed and torn into pieces	1 teaspoon granulated sugar
One 11-ounce can mandarin orange segments, drained	1 teaspoon light brown sugar
	1 clove garlic, finely chopped
½ cup (3 ounces) snow peas, strings removed	1 teaspoon finely chopped fresh ginger
⅓ cup finely chopped green onions	1 teaspoon grated orange zest
½ cup thinly sliced jicama strips	1 teaspoon soy sauce
½ cup cashews	1 teaspoon rice wine vinegar
Dressing	
3 tablespoons vegetable oil	White pepper

1. Prepare the salad: In a large bowl combine the watercress, mandarin oranges, snow peas, green onions, jicama, and cashews; toss gently.

2. Prepare the dressing: In a blender, mix the oil, orange juice, granulated and brown sugars, garlic, ginger, orange zest, soy sauce, and rice wine vinegar until smooth. Season to taste with white pepper.

3. Pour the dressing over the salad and toss gently until evenly coated. Serve immediately.

South of Her Border
if You Think You Can Afford Her

Spinach, Bacon, and Artichoke Salad *Serves 2*

2 cups (½ pound) fresh baby spinach leaves, washed	2 thin slices red onion
2 slices bacon, cooked and crumbled	1 ripe medium tomato, cut into wedges
2 hard-cooked eggs, sliced	Bottled honey mustard salad dressing, for serving
One 6-ounce jar marinated artichoke hearts, drained	Salt
	Freshly cracked black pepper

1. Divide the spinach between 2 salad plates. Sprinkle with the bacon. Arrange the egg slices, onion slices, artichoke hearts, and tomato wedges over the spinach. Season to taste with salt and pepper.

2. Pour the dressing over the salad and serve immediately.

Sensual Scenario: For this night you are a high-priced courtesan and your man will pay dearly for your pleasures. You are sultry, sexy, and expensive. Soft red light enhances the mood. You look like a million dollars and just might charge him as much. You show him a list of "services" you can perform, then dicker with him over the prices. Make sure he gets his money's worth. This could prove a profitable night for the both of you in addition to being loads of pleasure.

Cucumber Heaven

Cucumber, Tomato, and Feta Cheese Salad *Serves 2*

2 medium cucumbers, peeled, seeded, and sliced	Salt
	Freshly cracked black pepper
4 small red onion slices	
	Olive oil, for serving
⅓ cup whole pitted black olives	
	Red wine vinegar, for serving
⅓ cup crumbled feta cheese	Chopped fresh parsley, for garnish
1 small tomato, cut into wedges	Pickled peppers, for garnish

1. Arrange the cucumbers on 2 salad plates. Top with the onion, olives, feta cheese, and tomato wedges. Season to taste with salt and pepper.

2. Drizzle desired amounts of oil and vinegar over salads.

3. Garnish with parsley and pickled peppers.

4. Finish garnish with pickled pepper.

Waves of Pleasure

Crab and Avocado Salad with Exotic Fruit *Serves 2*

4 pineapple rings	1 tablespoon finely chopped celery
2 kiwis, peeled	1 tablespoon rice wine vinegar
6 ounces lump crabmeat, picked over, or lobster or shrimp	½ cup mayonnaise
1 mango, peeled, pitted, and chopped	Dash of ground cloves
1 finely chopped green onion	Salt
1 teaspoon grated lemon zest	White pepper
2 teaspoons lime juice	1 avocado, peeled and pitted
1 teaspoon finely chopped red bell pepper	2 cups gourmet salad greens
1 pickled jalapeño pepper, seeded and finely chopped	Nasturtium flowers (pesticide-free), for garnish

1. Chop 2 of the pineapple rings; set aside. Chop 1 of the kiwis and slice the second; set aside.

2. In a large bowl, combine the crabmeat, mango, chopped pineapple, chopped kiwi, green onion, lemon zest, lime juice, bell pepper, jalapeño pepper, celery, vinegar, mayonnaise, cloves, and salt and white pepper to taste. Toss gently, coating all ingredients. Cover and chill for at least ½ hour.

3. Arrange the salad greens on 2 dinner plates. Place the avocado halves on top of greens. Divide the crab mixture between the salads, mounding into the avocado halves and making sure some of the mixture overflows onto the plates.

4. Garnish the salad with the pineapple rings, sliced kiwi, and nasturtium flowers.

Serving Suggestion: This special and elegant salad can also be served as an appetizer or as an impressive lunch, so enjoy.

On the Side

Sides

Ménage à Trois 46

Que Bella Portabella 46

They Won't Make You Go Blind Carrots 47

Spear Me Asparagus 48

Don't Be Afraid of Alfredo 49

Stuffed Studly Spuds 49

Hole-in-One Harry 50

Kiss My Kabobs 51

I'm Just Wild about Saffron Potatoes 52

Ménage à Trois

Vegetable Medley *Serves 3*

1 tablespoon olive oil	1 clove garlic, finely chopped
½ medium onion, cut into julienne strips	1 teaspoon finely chopped fresh parsley
1 medium carrot, cut into julienne strips	Salt
1 small zucchini, cut into julienne strips	Freshly cracked black pepper
1 small yellow squash, cut into julienne strips	1 tablespoon thinly sliced fresh basil leaves, for garnish

1. Heat the oil in a large skillet, set over medium heat. Add the onion and carrot and cook for about 1 minute, or until slightly soft.

2. Add the zucchini, yellow squash, and garlic, and cook for 1 to 2 minutes, or until all the vegetables are tender.

3. Stir in the parsley. Season to taste with salt and pepper. Garnish with basil and serve.

Serving Suggestion: Satisfy your tastes by serving this dish to your lover, another male guest of your choosing, and yourself, or make him doubly happy and serve this dish to him, a female guest of his choosing, and yourself. As you can see, this provocative dish can swing both ways.

Que Bella Portabella

Portabello Mushrooms with Gorgonzola Cheese *Serves 2*

1 tablespoon olive oil	1 tablespoon red wine
½ onion, sliced	Salt
2 cloves garlic, finely chopped	Freshly cracked black pepper
8 ounces portabello mushrooms, sliced	Gorgonzola cheese, crumbled, for serving

1. Heat the oil in a large skillet set over medium heat. Add the onions and sauté for about 1 minute, or until slightly soft.

2. Add the garlic and sauté for about 1 minute, or until slightly soft.

3. Add the mushrooms and cook for about 2 minutes, or until vegetables are almost tender. Stir in the red wine. Season to taste with salt and pepper and mix well. Cook for about 30 seconds, or until the wine is reduced by one half.

4. Top with the crumbled Gorgonzola. Serve immediately.

They Won't Make You Go Blind Carrots
Baby Carrots with Brown Sugar *Serves 2*

1 cup (7 ounces) peeled baby carrots	2 teaspoons finely chopped fresh parsley
1½ teaspoons salted butter	Salt
1 clove garlic, finely chopped	
2 teaspoons light brown sugar	Freshly cracked black pepper

1. Bring a medium saucepan of water to a rapid boil. Add the carrots and cook for 3 to 5 minutes, or until fork-tender. Drain and keep warm.

2. Melt the butter in a medium saucepan set over low heat. Add the garlic and sauté for about 1 minute, or until tender. Add the brown sugar, parsley, and salt and pepper to taste. Stir well and cook for about 30 seconds, or until the sugar dissolves.

3. Stir in the cooked carrots, completely coating them with the sugar mixture. Serve immediately.

Sensual Scenario: Ask your doctor to examine you very carefully since you have a pain and don't know exactly where it hurts. See if your doctor can "diagnose" you. Tell him if he locates your ailment, you'll be his nurse for a day, attending to his every need.

Spear Me Asparagus

Asparagus Wrapped in Prosciutto *Serves 2*

8 to 10 asparagus spears	1 teaspoon lemon juice
2 teaspoons salted butter	Salt
2 teaspoons olive oil	Freshly cracked black pepper
1 teaspoon finely chopped shallots	2 slices prosciutto, for garnish
1 teaspoon Dijon mustard	Two 2-inch strips of canned pimientos, for garnish
2 tablespoons white wine	1 teaspoon grated lemon zest, for garnish

1. Bring a large saucepan of water to a rapid boil.

2. Prepare the asparagus by breaking off the woody ends of the stems and peeling most of the stalks up to the tender tips with a vegetable peeler.

3. Add the asparagus to the boiling water and cook for 2 to 4 minutes, or until crisp-tender. Drain the asparagus and set aside, keeping warm.

4. In the same pan, melt the butter with the oil over medium heat. Add the shallots, mustard, white wine, lemon juice, and salt and pepper to taste. Cook 1 to 3 minutes, or until sauce reduces by one third. Return the asparagus to the pan, stirring gently to coat with the butter mixture.

5. Evenly divide the asparagus between 2 plates. Pour the butter sauce over them. Wrap 1 prosciutto slice around the center of each asparagus bundle, tucking the ends under the bottom.

6. For garnish, arrange a pimiento strip over each prosciutto slice, bending it to resemble a ribbon. Sprinkle with lemon zest.

Don't Be Afraid of Alfredo
Fettuccine Alfredo *Serves 4*

8 ounces fettuccine	Salt
4 tablespoons salted butter	Freshly cracked black pepper
½ cup heavy cream	½ cup grated Parmesan or Romano cheese
4 ounces Fontina cheese, cut into cubes	1 tablespoon finely chopped fresh parsley, for garnish

1. Cook the fettuccine according to package directions. Drain and keep warm.

2. Melt the butter in a large saucepan set over medium heat. Add the cream and bring to a boil.

3. Stir in the Fontina cheese and reduce the heat to low. Cook 2 to 4 minutes, or until the mixture starts to thicken, stirring occasionally. Season to taste with salt and pepper. Stir in the Parmesan cheese. Remove from the heat.

4. Add the warm pasta to the sauce and toss well with two forks until well coated. Garnish with the parsley and serve immediately.

Stuffed Studly Spuds
Twice Baked Potatoes *Serves 2*

2 large russet potatoes, scrubbed	3 slices bacon, cooked and crumbled
½ teaspoon vegetable oil	¼ cup plus 2 teaspoons shredded Monterey Jack cheese
4 tablespoons salted butter	¼ cup plus 2 teaspoons shredded Cheddar cheese
1 leek (white part only), finely chopped	
1 clove garlic, finely chopped	Salt
5 tablespoons light cream	Freshly cracked black pepper
3 tablespoons sour cream	2 teaspoons finely chopped green onions, for garnish

1. Preheat the oven to 450°F.

2. Prick the potatoes with a fork and rub well with oil. Bake for 45 to 65 minutes, or until fork-tender.

3. Melt 1 tablespoon of the butter in a medium skillet set over medium heat. Add the leek and garlic and sauté for 3 to 5 minutes, or until soft. Set aside.

4. Remove the potatoes from the oven and let stand for 5 minutes or until cool enough to handle. Cut each potato carefully in half lengthwise. Scoop the pulp out of the potatoes and place in a bowl, making sure to leave a ¼-inch shell. Set aside the potato shells.

5. Add the leek mixture, light cream, sour cream, and the remaining 3 tablespoons butter to the potatoes in the bowl. With an electric hand-mixer, beat the potato mixture on medium speed until fluffy, but not completely smooth. By hand, blend in 2 tablespoons of the bacon, ¼ cup of the Monterey Jack cheese, and ¼ cup of the Cheddar cheese. Season to taste with salt and pepper.

6. Reduce the oven temperature to 375°F.

7. Fill the potato shells with the mashed potato mixture, and place them on a baking sheet. Bake for about 10 minutes, or until heated through.

8. Garnish with the green onions, remaining 2 teaspoons each Monterey and Cheddar cheeses, and crumbled bacon.

Hole-in-One Harry

Brussels Sprouts, Pearl Onions, and Cherry Tomatoes *Serves 2*

6 small Brussels sprouts, washed and outer leaves removed	1 teaspoon chopped fresh tarragon
6 pearl onions	1 teaspoon lemon juice
2 tablespoon butter	Salt
6 cherry tomatoes	Freshly cracked black pepper

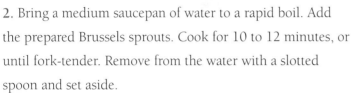

1. Make a shallow X-shaped cut into the bottom of each Brussels sprout with a paring knife.

2. Bring a medium saucepan of water to a rapid boil. Add the prepared Brussels sprouts. Cook for 10 to 12 minutes, or until fork-tender. Remove from the water with a slotted spoon and set aside.

3. Add the pearl onions to the boiling water. Cook for 3 to 5 minutes, or until fork-tender. Drain. When cool enough to handle, peel and set aside.

4. Melt the butter in a medium skillet. Add the cherry tomatoes, tarragon, and lemon juice. Cook for about 1 minute or until the tomatoes are heated through. Add the cooked Brussels sprouts and onions to the tomatoes. Stir gently, making sure all the vegetables are coated with the butter mixture. Season to taste with salt and pepper.

Sensual Scenario: Golfers love to have their egos stroked. So when you and Harry play hooky from work to spend a leisurely afternoon at the golf course, make sure you let Harry know how impressed you are with his putter. If you stroke his ego enough, Harry might even let you tee off. ❧

Kiss My Kabobs

Corn and Pepper Shish Kabobs *Serves 2*

2 small ears white or yellow corn, shucked	2 tablespoons salted butter
1 small onion, cut into 2-inch squares (about 8 pieces)	Salt
	Cayenne
1 small red bell pepper, cut into 2-inch squares (about 8 pieces)	2 teaspoons finely chopped fresh parsley, for garnish
1 small green bell pepper, cut into 2-inch squares (about 8 pieces)	

1. Trim ends off each ear of corn with a sharp knife. Cut each ear into thirds.

2. Bring a large saucepan of water to a rapid boil. Add the corn and cook for 3 to 5 minutes, or until tender. Remove the corn from the water with a slotted spoon and set aside.

3. Add the onion and bell peppers to the boiling water and cook for about 1 minute or until crisp-tender. Drain and set aside until cool enough to handle.

4. Melt the butter in a small saucepan set over low heat. Set aside.

5. With a metal skewer, carefully poke a small hole through each piece of corn. To assemble the kabobs, thread the onion, bell peppers, and corn onto bamboo skewers.

6. Pour the melted butter over the kabobs. Season to taste with salt and cayenne.

Sprinkle with parsley and serve.

I'm Just Wild about Saffron Potatoes
Saffron Potatoes *Serves 2*

2 cups canned chicken stock	6 new potatoes, scrubbed and cut in half
2 pinches saffron threads	
1 clove garlic, sliced	1 teaspoon finely chopped fresh parsley, for garnish

1. Bring the chicken stock to a boil in a medium saucepan set over high heat. Add 1 pinch of the saffron to the boiling stock. Cover and remove from the heat. Let stand for 4 minutes.

2. Return the chicken stock to a boil. Add the garlic and potatoes and cook for 13 to 15 minutes, or until the potatoes are fork-tender.

3. Remove the potatoes from the pan discarding the garlic and stock.

Garnish with the parsley and remaining pinch of saffron.

Don't Stop Now

Main Courses

One Hung Low Main Man......................58

I'm Goo Goo Ga Ga Over My Man............59

Touch Down Taco............................60

Beefcake 61

Oh My Cod! 62

Chick on a Bed of Roses....................63

Between the Sheets 64

Love Mussels 66

Love Me Tender.............................67

Titillating Breast of Chicken.............69

Chick on a Stick..........................70

Hot-to-Trot-A Enchilada...................71

Juicy Tails...............................72

One Hung Low Main Man
Pork Lo Mein *Serves 2*

¼ pound lo mein noodles	¾ cup (3 ounces) bean sprouts
2 tablespoon vegetable oil	
	2 teaspoons rice wine or dry sherry
¼ pound pork tenderloin, cut into ¼-inch pieces	
	1 tablespoon soy sauce
½ cup chopped yellow onion	
	1 tablespoon oyster sauce
1 clove garlic, finely chopped	
	¼ teaspoon granulated sugar
1 teaspoon fresh finely chopped ginger	
	2 tablespoons canned chicken stock
1 cup shredded Chinese cabbage (napa)	
	White pepper

1. Bring a large saucepan of water to a rapid boil. Add the lo mein noodles and cook until al dente. Drain and rinse in cold water. Set aside.

2. Heat 1 tablespoon of the oil in a wok or 12-inch nonstick skillet set over high heat. Add the pork and stir-fry for about 2 minutes, or until it is no longer pink. Remove from the wok and set aside.

3. Add the remaining 1 tablespoon oil to the wok. When hot, add the onion, garlic, and ginger, and stir-fry for about 1 minute, or until the onion begins to soften. Add the pork, cabbage, bean sprouts, and rice wine, and stir-fry for about 30 seconds, or until the flavors begin to blend. Put the cooked lo mein noodles on top of the vegetable-pork mixture.

4. In a small mixing bowl, mix the soy sauce, oyster sauce, sugar, chicken stock, and white pepper to taste. Pour over the noodles. Cover and cook for 1 minute. Uncover and stir. Serve immediately.

Serving Suggestions: This delectable dish is most authentic when eaten with chopsticks. Set out two pairs, and impress him with your expert handling of these slippery noodles

I'm Goo Goo Ga Ga Over My Man

Moo Goo Gai Pan *Serves 2*

½ pound boneless skinless chicken breasts, pounded	½ cup sliced mushrooms
2 tablespoons vegetable oil	1 teaspoon finely chopped fresh ginger
¾ cup chopped onion	¼ cup canned chicken stock
1 clove garlic, finely chopped	1 tablespoon rice wine or dry sherry
1 cup shredded Chinese cabbage, (napa)	½ teaspoon salt
¼ cup canned bamboo shoots, drained	½ cup (3 ounces) snow peas, strings removed
¼ cup canned sliced water chestnuts, drained	2 teaspoons cornstarch mixed with 2 teaspoons water
	White pepper

1. Slice the chicken into uniform strips; set aside.

2. Heat 1 tablespoon of the oil in a wok or large nonstick skillet set over high heat. Add the onion, garlic, cabbage, mushrooms, bamboo shoots, water chestnuts, and ginger, and stir-fry for about 30 seconds, or until the vegetables begin to soften. Add the chicken stock. Cover and cook for about 2 minutes, or until the vegetables are almost tender. Remove the vegetables from wok and keep warm.

3. Add the remaining 1 tablespoon oil to the wok. Add the chicken, rice wine, and salt, and stir-fry for about 2 minutes, or until chicken is no longer pink.

4. Return the cooked vegetables to the wok. Add the snow peas. Bring to a boil and stir in the cornstarch mixture. Cook until the sauce thickens. Season to taste with white pepper.

Serving Suggestions: This delicate, tender, and velvety dish goes well with steamed white rice. Your man might go goo goo ga ga over YOU for making such a special Chinese treat.

Touch Down Taco

Beef Tacos *Serves 2*

½ pound lean ground beef	Iceberg lettuce, shredded, for serving
½ chopped yellow onion	2 medium-sized ripe tomatoes, chopped, for serving
2 cloves garlic, finely chopped	
1 jalapeño or serrano pepper, finely chopped	Green onions, finely chopped, for serving
1 teaspoon ground cumin	Queso Fresco, crumbled, for serving (see Note)
Salt	Salsa, for serving
Cayenne	Four 7-inch flour tortillas

1. In a large nonstick skillet set over medium heat, cook and stir the ground beef for about 5 minutes, or until no longer pink. Drain any fat. Stir in the onion, garlic, and jalapeño peppers. Cook for 2 to 3 minutes, or until the vegetables are soft. Add the cumin, then salt and cayenne to taste.

2. Place the ground meat mixture, lettuce, tomatoes, green onions, cheese, and salsa in separate small serving bowls and arrange on the dining table.

3. Heat the flour tortillas according to the package instructions. Wrap in foil and then a towel to keep warm.

4. Assemble the tacos by dividing all the ingredients into fourths and spooning onto 1 side of each flour tortilla. Fold the tortillas in half and enjoy.

Note: Queso Fresco is a fresh Mexican cheese that can be purchased at Mexican specialty markets. Farmer's cheese can be substituted.

Sensual Scenario: Don't worry if your football hero makes a fumble while assembling his taco. Messy food can be fun, especially when eaten with your fingers. Think of how enjoyable the clean-up will be. Who knew tacos could be this tantalizing?

Beefcake

Peppery Creamy Filet Mignon *Serves 2*

1½ teaspoons freshly cracked black pepper	1 clove garlic, finely chopped
¼ teaspoon salt	6 small mushrooms
Two 6- to 8-ounce filet mignons, each about ¾ to 1 inch thick	2 tablespoons bourbon, brandy, or cognac
1 tablespoon vegetable oil	½ cup light cream
2 tablespoons finely chopped shallots	Fresh spinach leaves, for garnish

1. Rub pepper and salt into both sides of beef.

2. Heat the oil in a medium skillet set over high heat. Add the beef and cook for 2 to 3 minutes on each side for medium-rare. Remove the beef from the pan and keep warm. Reduce the heat to low.

3. Add the shallots, garlic, and mushrooms to the skillet and sauté for about 1 minute, or until soft. Add the bourbon and cream and stir for 1 to 2 minutes, or until the sauce slightly thickens.

4. Pour some of the sauce onto 2 serving plates and arrange a few spinach leaves on top. Place the beef on top of the spinach leaves and pour the remaining sauce and mushrooms over the top.

Sensual Scenario: Your mouth begins to water when you realize this Beefcake is your personal fitness trainer. You whet his appetite when he sees you in your sexy workout outfit, smelling squeaky clean and acting so positive and energetic. He can't wait to show you some new exercises. You remember how much it turns him on when he sees those tiny droplets of perspiration trickling down your toned body. It's time to sweat!

Oh My Cod!

Fish with Sweet Heat *Serves 2*

Two 6- to 7-ounces boneless fish filets such as cod, salmon, or sole	Lemon pepper
3 tablespoons salted butter, melted	2 tablespoons jalapeño jelly (see Note)
Onion powder	Garlic powder
2 tablespoons prepared mustard	Fresh dill, finely chopped
2 teaspoons lemon juice	Fresh parsley, finely chopped

1. Preheat the broiler. Grease a 9-inch baking dish.

2. Dip each fish filet in melted butter, coating well on both sides.

3. In a small bowl, mix the jalapeño jelly, mustard, and lemon juice. Season to taste with lemon pepper, onion powder, garlic powder, dill, and parsley. Smear the jelly mixture on both sides of the fish and place in the prepared baking dish.

4. Broil the fish 4 inches from heat source for about 4 minutes on each side, or until firm and cooked through but still moist.

Note: Jalapeño jelly can be purchased at Mexican specialty markets.

Serving Suggestion: This tasty sweet-heat fish-dish is further complemented by topping it with Honeydew This and Honeydew That Salsa (see page 30). Or, you might wish to try Go Man-Go Salsa (see page 31). Either salsa will capture your eyes as well as your taste buds. Oh My Cod! is quick, easy, and has heavenly visual appeal. He will worship you for making this unusual dish.

Sensual Scenario: You're soaking up the last of the late afternoon rays on a wide, sandy Cape Cod beach. You must've dozed off because when you sit up and look around, the once-bustling beach is completely deserted. You gaze at the ocean, still groggy from your nap, when a stranger arises from the surf. This incredibly sexy man walks toward you, and you shake your head to make sure you're not dreaming. You're not. You've heard there are many fish in the sea, but Oh My Cod!—this fish is the one for you.

Chick on a Bed of Roses

Chicken Breast with Rose Petal Mole (Moe-Lay) *Serves 2*

Chicken	2 cloves garlic, finely chopped
1 tablespoon vegetable oil	
2 boneless skinless chicken breast halves, pounded	½ teaspoon anise-flavored liqueur, or may substitute anise extract
2 tablespoons white wine	½ cup jarred roasted red peppers, drained
Salt	
Freshly cracked black pepper	1 medium pitaya, peeled and chopped (see Note)
Rose Petal Mole	⅓ cup white wine
6 red roses, pesticide-free	
1½ tablespoons salted butter	¼ cup water
¾ cup cashews	1 teaspoon honey
	Salt
2 tablespoons finely chopped shallots	Cayenne

1. Prepare the chicken: Heat the oil in a large nonstick skillet set over medium to high heat. Add the chicken breasts and sauté for 2 to 3 minutes on each side, or until a light golden brown. Add the wine, and salt and pepper to taste. Cook for 1 to 2 minutes, or until wine reduces by one half and the chicken is cooked through. Remove the chicken and keep warm.

2. Prepare the Rose Petal Mole: Carefully remove the petals from the roses. (Wear leather gloves to protect your hands from the prickly rose thorns.) Gently rinse the petals with water using care not to bruise the petals. Set aside the petals from 1 rose for garnish.

3. In the same skillet, melt the butter over medium heat. Add the garlic and shallots and sauté for about 30 seconds or until slightly cooked; remove from the heat and set aside.

4. In a food processor, grind the cashews on high speed to a fine powder. Reserve 2 tablespoons for garnish. Add the garlic mixture, liqueur, roasted red peppers, pitaya, wine, water, and honey

to the ground cashews in the food processor. Process until smooth. Season to taste with salt and cayenne. Add the rose petals and process until smooth.

5. Pour the Rose Petal Mole into the same skillet and cook over medium heat for 1 to 3 minutes, or until heated through. (Do not overcook. The flavors are very delicate and are at their peak only when warmed.) The sauce will thicken as it cooks. Remove from heat.

6. Pour some of the mole onto each serving plate and top with a chicken breast and a bit more mole. Garnish with the reserved ground cashews and rose petals. Exquisite!

Note: Pitaya is the fruit from the prickly pear cactus and can be purchased at Mexican specialty markets. One peach, peeled, pitted, and chopped can be substituted.

Serving Suggestion: A bouquet of long-stemmed red roses for a table centerpiece is a must.

Between the Sheets
Pasta and Polenta Beds with Red Pepper Sauce *Serves 2*

Red Pepper Sauce	
One 8- or 9-ounce jar roasted red peppers, drained	Two 3 x 5-inch pieces purchased plain polenta, cut about ½ inch thick (comes in tubes)
4 anchovy filets, drained	Salt
¼ teaspoon garlic powder	Freshly cracked black pepper
¼ teaspoon crushed red pepper	2 lasagna noodles, cooked
1 teaspoon olive oil	2 tablespoons grated Parmesan cheese
1 tablespoon finely chopped fresh parsley	2 thin slices prosciutto
Salt	4 tablespoons heavy cream, warmed
Freshly cracked black pepper	2 ravioli, cooked
Pasta and Polenta Beds 2 teaspoons olive oil	2 teaspoons thinly sliced fresh basil leaves, for garnish

1. Prepare the red pepper sauce: In a blender or food processor, purée the roasted red peppers, anchovies, garlic powder, crushed red pepper, olive oil, and parsley for 1 or 2 minutes, or until smooth. Season to taste with salt and pepper.

2. In a medium saucepan set over low heat, cook the red pepper sauce for 1 to 3 minutes, or until heated through; keep warm.

3. Prepare the polenta beds: Add 1 tablespoon of oil to a large nonstick skillet, on medium heat. Add the polenta, and season to taste with salt and pepper. Cook for 3 to 4 minutes on each side, or until golden brown and heated through. Place each piece of polenta on a dinner plate.

4. Trim the curly edge off one side of each lasagna noodle. Arrange 2 trimmed lasagna noodles lengthwise over each polenta bed. Adjust the noodles so the smooth trimmed edges meet in the center of the polenta and the ends touch the plate where possible. When adjusted, remove the lasagna noodles and set aside.

5. Sprinkle 1 tablespoon Parmesan cheese on top of each polenta bed. Lay 1 prosciutto slice on top of cheese. Top each bed with 2 tablespoons warm cream, spreading over entire surface and allowing some to drip down the sides.

6. Brush the lasagna noodles and raviolis with the remaining 1 teaspoon oil. Cover each bed with 2 lasagna noodles. Sprinkle the basil across the tops of the beds. Place the 2 raviolis on top of the basil on each bed to simulate pillows.

7. Very carefully spoon the warmed red pepper sauce on the plates all around the polenta beds. With a toothpick, draw starburst-type lines starting from the beds to the edges of the plates. This pulls the cream out through the sauce and makes a nice design. For more contrast, carefully drizzle more cream around the edge of the beds. Garnish with freshly cracked black pepper.

Serving Suggestion: This spectacular dish is worth the effort, so don't let the many steps intimidate you. It is really very simple to prepare. The surprise is twofold here. Basil is under your pillow for good luck, and several tasty surprises await you both . . . between the sheets.

Sensual Scenario: Play relaxing music and arrange candles everywhere to express a dreamy, romantic mood. Then serve this beautiful and delectable dinner in your sexiest nightie that always tells him you're ready for beddie. A sensuous yawn might also help him get the message. This is food for your wildest dreams. He'll be so impressed by your culinary efforts that you'll soon end up between the sheets.

Love Mussels
Mussels, Scallops, and Shrimp with Tomatoes *Serves 4*

2 tablespoons olive oil	½ teaspoon salt
1 cup finely chopped onion	½ teaspoon cayenne
5 cloves garlic, finely chopped	¼ teaspoon granulated sugar
One 28-ounce can whole plum tomatoes with juice	10 mussels, scrubbed and debearded
1 cup clam juice	10 sea scallops
¾ cup white wine	10 large shrimp, peeled and deveined
¼ cup orange juice	
¼ cup thinly sliced fresh basil leaves	½ cup (3 ounces) finely chopped ham
2 bay leaves	⅓ cup chopped fresh Italian parsley

1. Heat the oil in a Dutch oven set over medium heat. Add the onion and garlic and sauté for about 5 minutes, or until tender. Add the undrained tomatoes, clam juice, wine, orange juice, basil, bay leaves, salt, cayenne, and sugar. Break up the tomatoes into bite-size chunks with a spoon. Cook for about 10 minutes, or until the flavors meld, stirring occasionally.

2. Add the mussels, scallops, and shrimp. Cook covered for about 7 minutes, or until the mussels open. Stir once during cooking time. Discard any mussels that do not open. Discard the bay leaves. Gently stir in the ham and parsley. Serve immediately.

Serving Suggestions: Both of you will adore this sensuous meal. Serve this with crusty French or Italian bread and a salad. Mmm-mm, luscious. Good thing there will be leftovers for tomorrow night.

Sensual Scenario: Your fantasy is centered on the men at a Muscle Beach. The sun is beating down on your body while you groove to the tunes of your favorite music. Your Muscle Man will love you cooing over his bulging biceps. Offer to rub down his sore, overworked body with some nice lavender massage oil. Soon he'll be begging you to stroke his pecs. Remember to love his muscles.

Love Me Tender
Pork Tenderloin Roast with Cherry-Rosemary Sauce *Serves 6*

Pork Roast	Freshly cracked black pepper
One 2-pound pork tenderloin roast	
	Cherry-Rosemary Sauce
1 tablespoon olive oil	1 cup cherry preserves with whole cherries
Garlic powder	1 cup red wine
Salt	1½ tablespoons dried rosemary, crumbled

1. Prepare the pork roast: Preheat the oven to 375°F.

2. Rub the oil over the surface of the pork, coating well. Sprinkle with garlic powder, salt, and pepper to taste. Place in a roasting pan.

3. Roast the pork for 15 minutes. (This is about halfway through the total time.)

4. Prepare the Cherry-Rosemary Sauce: In a medium saucepan, combine the cherry preserves, red wine, and rosemary leaves, stirring well. Cook over low heat for 10 to 14 minutes, or until the alcohol has evaporated and the sauce slightly thickens, stirring occasionally. Remove from the heat and set aside.

5. When the pork has cooked for about 45 minutes, pour about one half of the Cherry-Rosemary Sauce on top. Continue cooking for 15 minutes or until a meat thermometer inserted into the thickest part of the meat reads 160°F. Remove from the oven and let stand, covered, for 5 minutes before carving.

6. Slice into ½-inch serving pieces and top with Cherry-Rosemary Sauce. Pass the remaining sauce.

Serving Suggestion: You might love this delicious and unusual sauce so much, you'll choose to make extra for passing. He'll think you were slaving all day in the kitchen to prepare this spectacular dish, but as you can see, it's as easy as magic. Let that be your secret.

Sensual Scenario: Elvis has entered the kitchen, and he is all shook up after he unzips your powder-blue, strapless fifties prom dress with his bedroom eyes. One look at your demure string of pearls, and one bite of your pork tenderloin is enough to convince the King that he just wants to be your teddy bear. When he swings his famous pelvis, it's all you can do not to swoon.

Titillating Breast of Chicken

Chicken Italiano with Broccoli and Mushrooms *Serves 2*

1 cup (½ pound) broccoli florets	½ teaspoon dried oregano leaves, crushed
2 boneless skinless chicken breast halves, pounded to ¼-inch thickness	2 tablespoons olive oil
	2 tablespoons salted butter
Salt	2 cloves garlic, finely chopped
Freshly cracked black pepper	2 tablespoons finely chopped onion
1 egg	⅓ cup sliced mushrooms
¼ cup all-purpose flour	¼ cup white wine
¼ cup grated Parmesan cheese	3 tablespoons lemon juice
½ teaspoon dried thyme leaves, crushed	Lemon slices, for garnish

1. Steam the broccoli until crisp-tender; set aside.

2. Season the chicken with salt and pepper to taste. Beat the egg in a small bowl. Combine the flour, Parmesan cheese, thyme, and oregano in another small bowl. Dip chicken into the beaten egg and then into the flour mixture, coating on both sides.

3. Heat the oil and butter in a large skillet set over medium-high heat. Add the coated chicken and cook for 2 to 3 minutes on each side or until golden brown and cooked through. Remove the chicken from the skillet and keep warm.

4. Add the garlic, onion, mushrooms, and steamed broccoli to the skillet and mix well, coating the vegetables with the pan drippings. Cook for 1 to 3 minutes, or until the vegetables are tender. Add the white wine and lemon juice and mix well.

5. Place the chicken on 2 dinner plates and top with the vegetable mixture.

Garnish with lemon slices and serve.

Chick on a Stick

Tropical Chicken Kabobs *Serves 2*

Sauce	1 teaspoon hot chile paste
One 8-ounce can apricot halves	(see Note)
1 teaspoon orange juice	**Kabobs**
	¾ pound boneless skinless chicken breasts,
1 teaspoon lime juice	cut into bite-size pieces
1 clove garlic	4 cherry tomatoes
1 teaspoon finely chopped fresh ginger	4 large pearl onions,
	peeled and parboiled
1 tablespoon soy sauce	
	½ medium fresh pineapple, peeled, cored,
1 tablespoon teriyaki sauce	and cut into 1-inch cubes
½ teaspoon rice wine vinegar	½ medium green bell pepper,
	cut into 4 squares
1 teaspoon light brown sugar	
	1 tablespoon olive oil
1 teaspoon honey	
	Salt
1 tablespoon red jalapeño jelly	
(see Note)	Freshly cracked black pepper

1. Preheat the broiler.

2. Prepare the sauce: Drain the apricots, reserving 1 tablespoon of the liquid. Combine the apricots and reserved liquid, orange juice, lime juice, garlic, ginger, soy sauce, teriyaki sauce, rice wine vinegar, brown sugar, honey, red jalapeño jelly, and chile paste in a blender or food processor and purée until smooth. Set aside.

3. Prepare the kabobs: Alternately thread the chicken, tomatoes, onions, pineapple, and bell pepper onto two 12-inch metal or bamboo skewers. (If using bamboo skewers, soak them in water 30 minutes before assembling the kabobs.) Brush the kabobs with the oil and season to taste with salt and pepper. Place on a broiler pan.

4. Broil the kabobs 4 inches from the heat source for 3 to 4 minutes. Turn over and brush with

the sauce, coating evenly. Broil for 3 or 4 minutes, or until the chicken is cooked through. Serve immediately.

Note: Jalapeño jelly can be purchased at Mexican specialty markets. Hot chile paste can be purchased at Asian specialty markets.

Serving Suggestion: Chick on a Stick is a beautiful and colorful dish. To add more flavor and variety, serve it with Go Man-Go Salsa (see page 31). The tropical fruit flavors teamed with the popular sweet heat elements are natural complements.

Sensual Scenario: You are both stranded on a deserted tropical island. You are playful and adventurous. The sounds of the ocean music and the smell of the tropical fruits put you in a relaxed mood. You look sexy in your island sarong. You love the idea of playing limbo with Island Man. See how low he can go. Whoever goes the lowest, wins. The winner gets full pampering privileges for one night.

Hot-to-Trot-A Enchilada
Cheese and Onion Enchiladas *Serves 4*

One 16-ounce jar enchilada sauce	5 cups shredded Monterey Jack and Cheddar cheeses, combined
Vegetable oil, for frying	
Eight 6- to 7-inch corn tortillas (use thicker variety if available)	Crema cacique Mexicana agrea, or sour cream (see Note), for serving
	Finely chopped green onions, for serving
1¾ cups of chopped yellow onions	Sliced black olives, for serving

1. Preheat the oven to 350°F. Grease a 14 x 10 x 2-inch baking pan.

2. Heat the enchilada sauce in a medium saucepan. Set over low heat until warm.

3. Heat 3 tablespoons oil in medium skillet set over medium-high heat. Add 1 tortilla to the pan and cook for about 1 minute on each side, or until soft. Use long-handled tongs to turn and remove the tortilla to several layers of paper towels to drain. Fry all the remaining tortillas, adding more oil to the skillet as necessary.

4. Dip a tortilla in the warm enchilada sauce, coating both sides. Generously fill with the cheeses and yellow onions. Roll up and arrange seam side down in prepared pan. Repeat with the remaining tortillas. Pour the remaining enchilada sauce on top of the enchiladas. Top with the remaining cheeses and yellow onions.

5. Cover the pan with foil. Bake for about 30 minutes, or until the cheese is melted and heated through.

Note: Crema cacique Mexicana agrea can be purchased at Mexican specialty markets.

Serving Suggestions: Top with crema cacique Mexicana agrea (or sour cream), green onions, and black olives.

Juicy Tails

Lobster Tails *Serves 2*

Two 6-ounce frozen lobster tails in the shells	1 tablespoon finely chopped fresh parsley
Melted salted butter, for basting and serving	Salt
2 whole lemons, cut in half	Freshly cracked black pepper

1. Thaw the lobster tails in refrigerator or in cold water.

2. Preheat the broiler.

3. Cut lobster shells lengthwise to the tails. Make another cut at the tails in opposite directions,

making a "T" and taking care to leave the tail attached. Brush well with the melted butter.

4. Broil the tails about 4 inches from heat source for 10 to 15 minutes, or until the flesh is slightly firm to the touch and cooked through. Baste with the melted butter several times during cooking.

5. Dip 2 lemon halves in the parsley and set aside for serving. Squeeze the remaining lemon halves over both tails. Season to taste with salt and pepper.

Serving Suggestion: Serve lobster tails with lemon and melted butter.

Lubrications

Beverages

Tropical Heat 78

Hot Tomato 78

Forbidden Fruit 79

Bottoms Up 79

Mucho Malo Mocha Java 80

Woo Woo 80

Creamy Wicked Willy 81

Float Johnson's Boat 81

French Kiss 82

Fancy Licker-ish 82

Main Squeeze 83

Slow Jimmy Fizz 83

Night Cap 84

Tropical Heat

Pineapple-Rum Cocktail *Serves 2*

1 medium pineapple	¼ cup lemon juice
2 shots dark rum	2 tablespoons lime juice
½ shot orange-flavored liqueur	½ cup ice cubes
1 cup orange juice	

1. Hollow out the pineapple, reserving 1 cup of the flesh and the leafy top.

2. In a blender, purée the reserved pineapple flesh with the rum, orange-flavored liqueur, orange juice, lemon juice, lime juice, and ice cubes until smooth.

3. Pour into the hollowed-out pineapple, and serve with 2 long straws. Garnish with the leafy top.

Hot Tomato

Bloody Mary *Serves 2*

2 cups tomato juice or vegetable juice	Worcestershire sauce
1 teaspoon steak sauce	3 shots vodka
2 teaspoons horseradish sauce	Ice
Hot pepper sauce	2 ribs celery, for garnish
Celery salt	Lemon wedges, for serving
Garlic powder	Lime wedges, for serving

1. In a pitcher, combine the tomato juice, steak sauce, and horseradish sauce. Stir well. Season to taste with hot pepper sauce, celery salt, garlic powder, and Worcestershire sauce. Add the vodka and stir well.

2. Fill 2 tall glasses with ice. Pour one half of the tomato juice mixture into each glass.

3. Garnish each glass with a celery rib. Squeeze the lemon and lime wedges in each glass before serving.

Forbidden Fruit
Strawberry, Blueberry, Mango, and Banana Smoothie *Serves 2*

1 cup frozen strawberries	½ banana, peeled
1 cup frozen blueberries	1¾ cups orange juice
½ mango, pitted and peeled	1 tablespoon honey

1. In a blender, purée the strawberries, blueberries, mango, banana, orange juice, and honey until smooth.

2. Pour into 2 medium glasses and serve immediately.

Bottoms Up
Frozen Daiquiri *Serves 2*

½ cup orange juice	2 teaspoons confectioners' sugar
¼ cup frozen limeade concentrate	1¾ shots light rum
½ shot lime juice	Ice cubes
2 tablespoons lemon juice	Lime slices, for garnish

1. In a pitcher, combine the orange juice, limeade concentrate, lime juice, lemon juice, confectioners' sugar, light rum, and ice cubes and stir well.

2. Strain and pour into 2 glasses. Garnish with lime slices.

Mucho Malo Mocha Java

Chocolate Coffee *Serves 2*

2 tablespoons heavy cream	1 tablespoon plus 1 teaspoon light brown sugar
1 teaspoon granulated sugar	1 cup whole milk
1 drop vanilla extract	Ground cinnamon, for garnish
¾ cup brewed strong coffee	Chocolate shavings, for garnish
1 ounce semisweet chocolate	Cinnamon sticks, for garnish

1. In a small bowl, combine the heavy cream, 1 teaspoon sugar, and vanilla extract. Beat until stiff. Set aside.

2. In the top of a double boiler over medium heat, combine the coffee, chocolate, and brown sugar. Stir occasionally until the chocolate melts. Whisk in the milk. Heat just until warm. Do not boil.

3. Pour into 2 large coffee cups and garnish with the whipped cream, ground cinnamon, chocolate shavings, and cinnamon sticks.

Woo Woo

Cranberry Peach Cocktail *Serves 2*

2 shots vodka	Ice
1 shot peach liqueur	Peach slices, for garnish
1 cup cranberry juice	

1. In a pitcher, combine the vodka, peach liqueur, and cranberry juice and stir well.

2. Strain and pour over ice in 2 tall glasses. Garnish with peach slices.

Creamy Wicked Willy

Chocolate-Chip Banana Frozen Smoothie *Serves 2*

2 large scoops of chocolate chip frozen yogurt or ice cream (see Note)	½ shot créme de cacao
½ banana, peeled	¼ shot banana-flavored liqueur
½ shot coconut-flavored rum	1½ cups milk
½ shot light rum	½ cup ice cubes
½ shot vodka	Chocolate chips, for garnish

1. In a blender, blend the frozen yogurt, banana, coconut-flavored rum, light rum, vodka, créme de cacao, banana-flavored liqueur, milk, and ice cubes until smooth. Bits of chocolate chips should still be visible.

2. Pour into 2 tall glasses and garnish with chocolate chips.

Note: Vanilla ice cream with 1 tablespoon of chocolate chips stirred in can be substituted for the frozen yogurt. 🌹

Float Johnson's Boat

Cherry Coke and Brandy Float *Serves 2*

4 medium scoops vanilla ice cream	Two 12-ounce cans cherry cola
2 shots brandy	Maraschino cherries, for garnish

1. In each of 2 tall ice cream float glasses, place 2 scoops ice cream.

2. Pour 1 shot brandy on top of the ice cream in each glass. Top off each float with 1 can cherry cola.

3. Garnish with maraschino cherries and serve with 2 very long straws.

Sensual Scenario: The year is 1956 and you are in an ice cream parlor flirting with Johnson. You think he's the cat's meow and intend to let him know. Fifties sock-hop dance tunes play on the jukebox. Your look is sweet yet smoldering in a skintight sweater, poodle skirt, and ponytail. He smells the brandy from the flask that you've smuggled in. You are so naughty and not just a little tipsy. The remainder of your night is spent rocking around the clock.

French Kiss

Champagne Cocktail *Serves 2*

2 teaspoons light brown sugar	½ shot brandy or cognac
4 drops bitters	
Champagne	Maraschino cherries, for garnish

1. Place 1 teaspoon brown sugar, 2 drops bitters, and ¼ shot brandy in each of 2 Champagne glasses.

2. Top with Champagne. Garnish with maraschino cherries and serve.

Fancy Licker-ish

Licorice Liqueur with Coffee Beans *Serves 2*

Licorice-flavored liqueur | Coffee beans

1. Pour licorice-flavored liqueur into 2 small-stemmed glasses.

2. Place an odd number of coffee beans in each glass. (The odd number is very good luck.)

Serving Suggestions: This is an Italian after-dinner treat, so it goes quite well with the Italian entrées in this book. Try it after your Titillating Breast of Chicken or Between the Sheets (see page 69 and page 64).

Main Squeeze

Screwdriver *Serves 2*

1¾ shots vodka	Ice
2 cups orange juice	Orange slices, for garnish
¼ cup pink grapefruit juice	

1. In a pitcher, combine the vodka, orange juice, and grapefruit juice and stir well.

2. Pour over ice in 2 tall glasses. Garnish with orange slices.

Slow Jimmy Fizz

Sloe Gin Fizz *Serves 2*

3 shots sloe gin	Ice
3 tablespoons lemon juice	Club soda
2 teaspoons confectioners' sugar	Fresh raspberries, for garnish
1 teaspoon raspberry-flavored liqueur	Fresh mint leaves, for garnish

1. In a pitcher, combine the sloe gin, lemon juice, confectioners' sugar, and raspberry-flavored liqueur and stir well.

2. Pour into 2 tall glasses that are filled halfway with ice cubes. Fill up glasses with club soda. Garnish with raspberries and mint leaves.

Serving Suggestion: The deep ruby-red color of this beautiful cocktail will be a refreshing change of pace. Try it in the summertime or when Jim gets a little too warm. Don't let Jim fizzle out!

Night Cap

Milk Laced with Rum *Serves 2*

2 cups whole milk	Ice
2 shots dark rum	Ground nutmeg, for garnish
2 teaspoons confectioners' sugar	Cinnamon sticks, for garnish

1. In a pitcher combine the milk, dark rum, and confectioners' sugar and stir well.

2. Pour into 2 medium glasses filled with ice. Garnish with a dash of ground nutmeg and cinnamon stick.

Sweet Seductions

Desserts

Shameless Tart 90

Bananas Faster, Faster 91

Puh-lease Officer, Give Me More 92

Tarzan's Chocolate-dipped Banana with Nuts 93

Artful Andy 94

Luscious Lips 96

Icy Seduction 97

I Scream for His Ice Cream 98

Chill Your Hot Banana 99

Peachy Pleasures 100

Frozen Suckers 100

"Yes, You Can" Flan 101

Tear My Suit Off 102

Strawberries Moan-an-off 103

Randy Candy 104

Shameless Tart

Apple Pear Tart *Serves 6*

Tart	1 teaspoon vanilla extract
One 20- to 25-ounce jar sweetened applesauce	One 9-inch pastry shell
½ cup apricot preserves	**Glaze**
	⅓ cup apricot preserves
3 tablespoons salted butter	2 teaspoons water
1 teaspoon apple-, pear-, or orange-flavored liqueur	1 teaspoon apple-, pear-, or orange-flavored liqueur
¾ pound tart apples, peeled, cored, and sliced ¼ inch thick	2 teaspoons lemon juice
¾ pound pears, peeled, cored, and sliced ¼ inch thick	Vanilla ice cream, for serving

1. Prepare the tart: Preheat the oven to 375°F.

2. Cook the applesauce in a medium saucepan set over medium heat, stirring frequently, for 9 to 12 minutes, or until reduced to 2 cups. Stir in the apricot preserves and 1 tablespoon of the butter. Remove from the heat and stir in the vanilla and apple-flavored liqueur. Cool for 5 minutes.

3. Combine the apple and pear slices and lemon juice in a medium bowl and mix well.

4. Pour the applesauce mixture into the pie shell. Arrange the apple and pear slices alternately on top of the applesauce mixture.

5. In a small saucepan, melt the remaining 2 tablespoons butter. Pour the butter evenly over the apples and pears.

6. Bake for 35 minutes or until the fruit is fork-tender and light golden brown.

7. Prepare the glaze: In a small saucepan set over medium heat, cook the apricot preserves, water, and apple-flavored liqueur, and cook for 1 to 3 minutes, or until the glaze begins to melt. Immediately pour glaze over the baked tart, coating fruit completely. Serve warm with scoops of vanilla ice cream.

Sensual Scenario: The lord of the English manor requests the presence of his housemaid to attend to his every whim. Your appearance is typical maid attire with a black uniform, white apron, and upswept hair. Dim the lights, brew some tea, and set out freshly cut lavender flowers to fill the air. Your stilted, reserved, and proper attitude is only a façade, because your lord is about to be served a very tasty Shameless Tart. You strip down to your garter belt and black stockings just in time to serve tea. The remains of the day are spent with Big Ben. 🌹

Bananas Faster, Faster

Bananas Foster *Serves 2*

1 tablespoon unsalted butter	2 large, firm bananas, peeled and halved lengthwise
2 tablespoons orange juice	
2 tablespoons light brown sugar	1 teaspoon vanilla extract
½ teaspoon grated orange zest	1 shot orange-, cherry-, or apple- flavored liqueur
½ teaspoon grated lemon zest	or rum

1. Melt the butter in a medium skillet set over medium heat. Add the orange juice, brown sugar, and orange and lemon zests, and cook for 1 to 2 minutes, or until the sugar melts.

2. Add the bananas and stir gently to coat with the sauce. Cook for 1 minute, or until heated through. Remove from the heat and stir in the vanilla extract.

3. Sprinkle with liqueur and ignite with a long match. Have a lid handy to smother the flame if needed. Serve immediately.

Sensual Scenario: It's the perfect day to take your brand new candy-apple-red convertible for its virgin spin. The wind blows through your hair and your scarf whips behind you as you accelerate, shifting smoothly into a higher gear. Uh-oh, a siren—should you slow down and behave or speed up for the chase? One glimpse of your studly pursuer is all you need to make that decision. You ease to a stop and watch him saunter slowly toward you. Slow is nice, but you'd rather he go faster, faster.

Puh-lease Officer, Give Me More

Chocolate Mousse with Raspberry Sauce *Serves 4*

Raspberry Sauce	1 tablespoon unsalted butter,
5 ounces frozen raspberries,	cut into pea-sized pieces
thawed and drained	
	½ teaspoon vanilla extract
2 tablespoons water	
	2½ tablespoons granulated sugar
1 tablespoon cranberry juice	
	¾ cup heavy cream
1 teaspoon light rum	
	Fresh raspberries, for garnish
1½ tablespoons lemon juice	
	Fresh mint leaves,
1½ tablespoons granulated sugar	for garnish
Chocolate Mousse	Semisweet chocolate shavings,
4 ounces semisweet chocolate	for garnish

1. Prepare the raspberry sauce: In a small saucepan set over medium heat, combine the raspberries, water, and cranberry juice. Bring to a boil, stirring occasionally. Remove from the heat.

2. In a food processor or blender, purée the raspberry mixture, rum, lemon juice, and sugar. Strain the raspberry purée through a fine sieve, into a small bowl. Cover and refrigerate overnight.

3. Prepare the chocolate mousse: Melt the chocolate in the top of a double boiler over gently boiling water. Stir until smooth. Whisk in the butter until smooth and blended. Add the vanilla and sugar, and stir until smooth. Remove the pan from the boiling water and let cool.

4. In a deep, medium bowl, beat the cream until stiff. Gently fold half of the whipped cream into the cooled chocolate mixture. Fold the remaining whipped cream into the mixture. Cover and refrigerate for about 1 hour or until set.

Serving Suggestion: Spread a small pool of raspberry sauce onto dessert plates. Top with a large spoonful of the chocolate mousse. Arrange a small mound of the raspberries at the base of the mousse. Garnish with a few fresh mint leaves tucked under the raspberries and scatter chocolate shavings on top of the mousse.

Sensual Scenario: You are a law-abiding citizen, but must be punished when you are discovered indulging in this illegal dessert. Your policeman catches you breaking the law by eating your mousse in the nude. And you weren't using any silverware! Your officer approaches, prepared to arrest and handcuff you, but he soon joins in when he realizes how fun it is to use your hands.

Tarzan's Chocolate-dipped Banana with Nuts
Chocolate-dipped Banana on a Stick *Serves 2*

2 long, large, firm bananas, peeled	Finely chopped nuts for dipping (such as cashews, pistachios, or peanuts)
5 ounces semisweet chocolate	

1. Insert a wooden frozen-treat stick into 1 end of each banana, creating handles.

2. Melt the chocolate in the top of a double boiler over gently boiling water. While it is melting, pour chopped nuts onto a large plate.

3. Stir chocolate until smooth, and pour it onto a large plate. Dip the bananas into the chocolate, turning gently to coat.

4. Immediately roll the chocolate-coated bananas in the chopped nuts, turning gently to coat well.

5. Place on waxed-paper-lined plate and freeze for 1 to 2 hours, or until firm.

Sensual Scenario: He Tarzan, you Jane. Your daring spirit perfectly complements the primal bravado of your strong, silent lover. Create a setting that reveals you are in a tropical paradise. Tarzan loves you scantily clothed, with a jungle orchid adorning your wild long locks. His loincloth barely covers him. Being the nature boy that he is, he would prefer to be nude, but you urge him to be somewhat civilized. You and Tarzan are in jungle heaven.

Artful Andy

Edible Body Paints *Serves 2*

Orange Orbit	2 teaspoons frozen orange juice
1 cup prepared vanilla pudding	concentrate

(In a small bowl, combine the pudding and orange juice concentrate and mix well.)

Strawberry Sin	Fresh strawberries, for garnish
One 16-ounce jar strawberry glaze	
	Fresh cherries, for garnish
Banana Sauce	
1 cup prepared banana pudding	Chocolate chips, for garnish
Chocolate Glide	Canned mandarin oranges, for garnish
One 16-ounce container chocolate topping	
(preferably in squeeze bottle)	Banana slices, for garnish
Creamy Cream	Fresh mint leaves, for garnish
One 16-ounce can	
aerosol whipped cream	3 paintbrushes

Serving Suggestion: Fill small attractive bowls with the puddings. Be sure to have towels handy for clean-up because this is a very messy dessert.

All you need is a clean, bare body for your canvas. Let your imagination go, and watch those creative juices flow.

Sensual Scenario: Ask Andy if he will be the canvas first. He'll surely be impressed with your brush strokes and artistic ability. Don't forget to use the beautiful natural garnishes to adorn your canvas. A sprinkle of chocolate chips here, a strawberry with orange slices there. . . . Have fun drizzling the chocolate glide straight from the bottle onto your canvas. Be adventurous. Try your hand at finger painting.

Luscious Lips

Lip-shaped Raspberry Cream Tart *Serves 2*

2 refrigerated pie crusts	¾ cup Raspberry Sauce (See Puh-lease Officer, Give Me More, Page 92)
1 pint raspberries or one 10-ounce package frozen dry-pack raspberries, thawed	Aerosol whipped cream
	Fresh raspberries, for garnish
2 tablespoons raspberry-flavored liqueur	Confectioners' sugar, for garnish
1 tablespoon orange-flavored liqueur	Fresh mint leaves, for garnish

1. Preheat the oven to 375°F.

2. Unfold the pie crusts and press gently to flatten. Cut out a 6 x 4-inch lip shape from heavy paper. Place the lip pattern on 1 pie crust. Cut around the pattern with a paring knife. Repeat the process to form 4 lip-shaped pastries.

3. Arrange the pastries on a greased baking sheet, with a large spatula. Bake for 13 to 18 minutes, or until the pastries begin to turn a light golden color. Remove from the baking sheet with a large spatula and transfer to a cooling rack until they cool completely.

4. In a small bowl, combine the raspberries, raspberry-flavored liqueur, and orange-flavored liqueur and mix gently.

5. Generously apply red lipstick to your lips. Carefully kiss around the rims of 2 dessert plates.

6. Spread a small pool of raspberry sauce in the center of each plate. Top the sauce on each plate with 1 lip pastry. Carefully squeeze the whipped cream along the edges of the lip pastry, forming a border. Spoon the raspberries in the center of the pastry and cover with a second lip pastry.

7. Pour raspberry sauce over the top pastry, allowing it to drizzle down the sides. Sprinkle with sifted confectioners' sugar for garnish. Mound a few fresh raspberries at the base and tuck a few mint leaves under the raspberries.

Serving Suggestion: Don't forget to wear the same color lipstick when serving this dish and smile. I wouldn't be surprised if this dish gives him ideas when he sees all these luscious lips! 🌹

Icy Seduction
Champagne Freeze *Serves 4*

1 bottle Champagne, 750ml	½ cup superfine sugar
	Strawberries, for garnish
6 egg whites, at room temperature (see Note*)	Mint leaves, for garnish

1. Pour ½ of the Champagne into a medium glass bowl. Cover and place in freezer.

2. In a large glass bowl, beat the egg whites and sugar on high until they form stiff peaks. Cover and place in the freezer.

3. Pour some of the remaining Champagne in a stemmed glass, sip, and relax.

4. Freeze both mixtures for 1 to 2 hours, or until fairly frozen.

5. Using a fork, break up both mixtures into medium-fine ice crystals and return to freezer.

6. Pour another glass of Champagne, and relax for 1 hour.

7. Remove both mixtures from the freezer. Using a spatula, gently fold the Champagne into the egg whites, making sure to leave the delicate texture of the meringue intact.

Serving Suggestion: Fill stemmed Champagne glasses with the icy Champagne. Garnish with strawberries and mint leaves.

Note: Since this is frozen, the alcohol content is at full strength.

*Note: Because of the slight risk of salmonella, raw eggs should not be served to the very young, the ill or elderly, or to pregnant women. 🐦🦢

I Scream for His Ice Cream
Peppered Strawberries on Ice Cream *Serves 2*

2 tablespoons unsalted butter	1 teaspoon freshly cracked black pepper
3 tablespoons granulated sugar	1 pint strawberries, sliced
½ cup orange juice	1 shot brandy or cognac
3 tablespoons lemon juice	Premium vanilla ice cream

1. Melt the butter in a large skillet set over medium heat. Add the sugar and cook, stirring constantly, for 2 to 4 minutes, or until caramelized. Stir in the orange juice, lemon juice, and pepper.

2. Add the strawberries and cook for about 1 minute, or until heated through and liquid turns red.

3. Add brandy and ignite with a long match. Have a lid handy to smother the flame if needed. When the flame dies out, serve over ice cream.

Sensual Scenario: On a sultry summer afternoon, when your body is slick with sweat and there's no pool in sight, something to cool you down would be perfect. Suddenly, you hear the music of an ice cream truck driving down your street. From your window you see a young, buff Ice Cream Boy, and you get even hotter. He's obviously attracted to you. He shows you what he's selling, and in no time you are screaming for his ice cream! 🌹🦢

Chill Your Hot Banana

Honey-drizzled Banana Fritters Served over Ice Cream *Serves 2*

Vegetable oil, for frying	⅓ cup whole milk
½ cup all-purpose flour	1 tablespoon unsalted butter, melted
1 tablespoon granulated sugar	
1 teaspoon baking powder	2 large firm bananas, peeled
⅛ teaspoon salt	Premium vanilla or banana ice cream
1 egg, beaten	Honey, for drizzling

1. Fill a deep, heavy-bottomed, medium-sized saucepan with 2 inches of oil. Heat the oil over medium heat until it reaches 375°F.

2. In a medium bowl, sift together the flour, sugar, baking powder, and salt.

3. Measure 2 tablespoons of the beaten egg and pour into a small bowl. Discard the remaining egg. Stir in the milk and butter.

4. Stir the liquid ingredients into the flour mixture and mix well until smooth and blended. Add more milk or flour as needed to make the batter the proper consistency for completely coating the bananas.

5. Slice the bananas lengthwise and then into thirds. Dip bananas into the batter. Carefully add the bananas to the hot oil. Fry for 3 or 4 minutes, or until golden brown, turning once during cooking. Drain the fritters on paper towels.

6. Serve the hot fritters over ice cream and drizzle generously with honey.

Sensual Scenario: As an award-winning archaeologist, your lover's work takes him all over the world. Today he happens to be in the Sahara desert in the middle of an especially long dig. He is taking a break from the intense heat in the shade of a billowing tent. You enter the tent wearing a sheer, gauzy gown and holding a bucket of ice cubes. You drag one lightly across his overheated skin and tell him, "I've come to Chill Your Hot Banana."

Peachy Pleasures

Peach Sorbet *Serves 4*

4 large peaches, peeled and pitted

2 tablespoons lemon juice

1 tablespoon orange juice

1 tablespoon peach preserves

1 teaspoon orange- or peach-flavored liqueur

Peach slices, for garnish

Fresh mint leaves, for garnish

1. Cut the peaches into chunks. Toss with the lemon and orange juices and preserves. Place on a plate, cover with plastic wrap, and freeze until solid.

2. In a food processor, process frozen fruit, stopping frequently to scrape down the sides of the bowl. The fruit should form medium-fine crystals. Add the orange-flavored liqueur and process until smooth and fairly firm.

3. Serve immediately or store in a covered bowl in the freezer for up to 1 day.

4. Garnish with peach slices and mint leaves.

Serving Suggestion: This dessert looks beautiful when served in a stemmed glass with a doily liner beneath it.

Frozen Suckers

Berry Frozen Juice Treats *Serves 4*

1 cup mixed frozen unsweetened berries (raspberries, strawberries, and blueberries)

1½ tablespoons orange juice

1½ teaspoons lemon juice

2 tablespoons frozen mixed-berry or cranberry juice concentrate, thawed

2 tablespoons granulated sugar

1. In a food processor or blender, combine the frozen berries, sugar, orange and lemon juices, and berry juice concentrate. Blend until smooth.

2. Pour into individual frozen-treat molds and freeze for about 1 hour, or until just beginning to set. Insert wooden frozen-treat sticks and freeze until completely solid.

"Yes, You Can" Flan
Flan with Slivered Almonds *Serves 6*

½ cup granulated sugar	1 teaspoon vanilla extract
One 14-ounce can sweetened condensed milk	Slivered almonds, for garnish
1½ cups whole milk	Edible flowers (pesticide-free violas, pansies, or mini carnations), for garnish
5 eggs	

1. Preheat oven to 350°F.

2. In a metal 9 x 5 x 3-inch loaf pan, cook the sugar over low heat for about 5 minutes, or until caramelized. Using oven mitts, carefully hold the pan edges and rotate so the sugar melts evenly and coats the bottom and sides of the pan. Remove the pan from the heat and cool.

3. In a blender, combine the condensed milk, whole milk, eggs, and vanilla until thoroughly mixed.

4. Pour the milk mixture into the caramelized loaf pan. Cover with foil and place in a larger baking pan. Place on the oven rack and pour about 1 to 2 inches of hot water into the larger pan. Bake for about 1 hour, or until a knife inserted into the center of the flan comes out clean.

5. Place the almonds on a baking sheet. Bake for 5 to 7 minutes, or until golden brown. (You may do this step toward the end of the flan baking time.)

Serving Suggestions: This dish is best served chilled. Chill in the refrigerator for several hours or overnight. Before inverting, run a sharp knife around the edges of the pan to loosen the flan. To serve, place a large serving platter over the flan. Carefully and quickly invert the pan, allowing the caramel to run down the sides of the flan. Sprinkle with slivered almonds and garnish with a few edible flowers.

Tear My Suit Off

Tiramisu *Serves 8*

¼ cup confectioners' sugar	2 tablespoons coffee-flavored liqueur
½ cup granulated sugar	1 tablespoon cognac
3 egg yolks	¾ cup brewed espresso or very strong coffee
1¼ pounds Mascarpone cheese (see Note)	18 ladyfingers
1 tablespoon hazelnut-flavored liqueur	Cocoa powder, for garnish
1 tablespoon almond-flavored liqueur	Coffee beans, for garnish

1. In a mixing bowl, whisk the sugars and egg yolks until smooth. Add the Mascarpone cheese, liqueurs, and cognac and beat until fluffy.

2. Pour the cheese mixture into the top of a double boiler and cook over boiling water on high heat for 4 minutes, stirring occasionally. Remove from the heat.

3. Line an 8-inch springform pan with plastic wrap. Spread about one-third of the cheese mixture in the bottom of the pan.

4. Pour the espresso into a medium bowl. Soak 9 of the ladyfingers, 1 at a time, in the coffee. Arrange the soaked ladyfingers over the cheese in the bottom of the pan. Spoon another one-third of the cheese mixture on top, spreading evenly. Sprinkle with the cocoa powder. Soak the remaining 9 ladyfingers in the espresso and arrange over the cocoa. Top with the remaining one-third cheese mixture, spreading evenly. Sprinkle with cocoa. Cover and refrigerate overnight.

5. Remove the side of the springform pan and invert onto a serving plate. Carefully remove the bottom of the pan. Sprinkle with cocoa and garnish with coffee beans.

Note: Mascarpone cheese can be purchased at Italian specialty markets.

Sensual Scenario: You are alone in the gorgeous resort city of Taormina in Sicily, and you're sipping a glass of red wine at an outdoor café overlooking the beautiful blue Mediterranean Sea. The breeze from the water caresses your skin, and you feel very beautiful. A handsome man approaches you and offers you an enormous amount of money to be his private masseuse for one night. You are in just the right mood to say yes. You go to his villa, then realize you don't even know his name. But as he disrobes, you realize it doesn't matter. . . .

Strawberries Moan-an-off
Strawberries Romanoff *Serves 2*

1 pint large strawberries, leaves attached	Sour cream, for serving
	Light brown sugar, for serving

1. Wash the strawberries and gently pat dry.

2. Mound the sour cream in a small serving bowl.

3. Spoon the brown sugar into another small serving bowl, breaking up any lumps.

4. Place the bowls of sour cream and brown sugar in the center of a beautiful large serving platter. Arrange the strawberries around the bowls.

Serving Suggestion: Dip the strawberries first in the sour cream, then in the brown sugar, and enjoy. This is a very simple yet elegant dessert. You'll surely impress him, especially if you feed him the double-dipped Moan-an-off.

Randy Candy

White and Dark Chocolate-dipped
Fruit and Snacks *Serves 4*

5 ounces semisweet chocolate	Assorted dried fruit (apricots, pineapple, banana chips)
5 ounces white chocolate	Pretzel sticks
Fresh strawberries, washed and dried	

1. Melt the semisweet and white chocolates separately and place in 2 bowls.

2. Dip the strawberries, assorted dried fruits, and pretzels in the melted chocolates.

3. Place on waxed paper and let stand until the chocolate hardens.

Serving Suggestions: These make very nice candy alternatives. They are also a perfect way to finish a dinner with a light dessert.

The Morning After

Breakfast

Stud-a-Muffin 110

Quiche Him Good Morning 111

Hot Buns 112

Hot Cherry Turn Her Over 113

Peter, Peter Pumpkin Eater 113

Surprise Me Frenchy Toast 114

Stud-a-Muffin

Eggs Benedict *Serves 2*

Eggs Benedict	2 egg yolks, beaten
2 English muffins, split	⅛ teaspoon salt
4 slices Canadian bacon	Dash cayenne
½ teaspoon vegetable oil	1 tablespoon lemon juice
4 poached eggs	Sliced black olives, for garnish
Hollandaise Sauce ¼ pound (1 stick) salted butter	Fresh chives, finely chopped, for garnish

1. Prepare the Eggs Benedict: Butter the English muffin halves and toast.

2. Heat the oil in a small skillet set over medium heat. Add the Canadian bacon and cook for about 1 minute on each side, or until warmed.

3. Place 1 piece of Canadian bacon on each toasted English muffin half. Top with the poached eggs.

4. Prepare the Hollandaise Sauce: Melt the butter in a small saucepan set over medium heat until bubbly.

5. In a blender, blend the egg yolks, salt, cayenne, and lemon juice on high speed. With the blender running, slowly add the melted butter in a steady stream.

6. Pour the sauce mixture into a saucepan and cook over low heat for about 30 seconds, or until reheated, stirring constantly. Immediately pour sauce over the eggs. Garnish with black olives and chives.

Quiche Him Good Morning

Bacon and Spinach Quiche *Serves 4*

1 cup shredded Monterey Jack cheese	3 cloves garlic, finely chopped
1 cup shredded Swiss cheese	One 10-ounce package frozen chopped spinach, thawed and squeezed dry
2 tablespoons all-purpose flour	
One 9-inch pastry shell	6 eggs, well beaten
6 slices bacon, cooked and crumbled	1 cup whole milk
1½ tablespoons salted butter	Salt
½ cup chopped onion	Cayenne

1. Preheat the oven to 400°F.

2. In a medium bowl, combine the Monterey Jack and Swiss cheeses and the flour; toss well. Pour into pastry shell, distributing evenly. Sprinkle the bacon evenly over the cheeses.

3. Melt the butter in a medium skillet set over medium heat. Add the onion and garlic and cook for 1 to 3 minutes, or until soft. Spoon evenly over the filling in the pastry shell. Top with the spinach, distributing evenly.

4. In a medium bowl, whisk the eggs and milk until well mixed. Season to taste with salt and cayenne. Pour over the filling in the pastry shell. Use a fork to gently swirl the filling so the egg mixture reaches the bottom of the pan.

5. Bake for 10 minutes. Carefully remove from the oven. Reduce the oven temperature to 375°F. Cover the edges of the pastry with foil to prevent over-browning. Return the quiche to the oven. Bake for 40 minutes, or until a knife inserted into center comes out clean.

Serving Suggestion: This is such a delicious morning-after meal—all you need to complete it is fresh fruit, juice, and coffee. Make sure you smile real pretty when you Quiche Him Good Morning.

Hot Buns

Cinnamon Sticky Buns *Serves 4*

½ cup granulated sugar	One 12-ounce can refrigerated biscuits
1 tablespoon ground cinnamon	¼ pound (1 stick) salted butter, melted

1. Preheat the oven to 400°F.

2. In a small bowl, combine the sugar and cinnamon and mix well; set aside.

3. Cut each refrigerator biscuit into quarters.

4. Pour the melted butter into a 9-inch round baking pan or pie pan. Place the biscuit quarters in the baking pan, turning to coat all edges with the butter. Sprinkle with the cinnamon-sugar mixture.

5. Bake for 9 to 12 minutes, or until a light golden brown.

Hot Cherry Turn Her Over

Hot Cherry Turnover *Serves 4*

2 refrigerated pie crusts	1 tablespoon salted butter, melted
One 16-ounce can cherry pie filling	4 teaspoons granulated sugar

1. Preheat the oven to 400°F.

2. Cut each circle of pie crust dough in half. Place on a floured surface and press gently to flatten and smooth out, making sure any tears are pinched closed.

3. Spoon about ¼ to ⅓ cup cherry pie filling on 1 side of each half circle of pie crust dough. Brush the edges of the dough with water. Fold the other side of the dough over the filling, pinching the edges together.

4. Place the turnovers on a buttered baking sheet. Brush with melted butter and sprinkle 1 teaspoon of sugar over each. Bake 9 to 12 minutes, or until golden brown.

Peter, Peter Pumpkin Eater

Pumpkin Coffee Cake *Serves 8*

4 eggs, beaten	One 18-ounce yellow cake mix
One 16-ounce can pumpkin purée	One 14-ounce can sweetened condensed milk
¾ cup granulated sugar	
2 teaspoons ground cinnamon	½ pound (2 sticks) salted butter, melted
1 teaspoon pumpkin pie spice	1 cup chopped pecans

1. Preheat the oven to 350°F.

2. In a large bowl, beat the eggs, sweetened condensed milk, pumpkin, sugar, cinnamon, and pumpkin pie spice until well mixed.

3. Pour into an ungreased 13 x 9-inch baking pan. Sprinkle the dry cake mix over the top. Use a knife to swirl the cake mix and pumpkin mixture together. Drizzle with the melted butter and sprinkle the pecans on top.

4. Bake for 45 to 50 minutes, or until a toothpick inserted in the center of the cake comes out clean. Serve warm.

Serving Suggestion: This is a very delicious and simple coffee cake to make for your man the morning after. Try serving this with fresh fruit, juice, and coffee. No doubt you are tired from last night, so this recipe will be a snap to prepare.

Surprise Me Frenchy Toast
Stuffed French Toast with
Fruit Syrup *Serves 2*

French Toast	8 slices white or wheat bread
8 ounces cream cheese, softened at room temperature	2 tablespoons vegetable oil
¼ cup confectioners' sugar	**Berry Syrup** 1 cup maple syrup
1 teaspoon grated orange zest	⅓ cup fresh or frozen strawberries, blueberries, raspberries, or pitted Bing cherries
4 eggs, beaten	
½ cup milk	**Orange Syrup** 1 cup maple syrup
1 teaspoon granulated sugar	1 tablespoon orange marmalade
½ teaspoon ground cinnamon	⅓ cup canned mandarin oranges, drained
¾ teaspoon vanilla extract	

1. Prepare the French toast: In medium bowl, stir together the cream cheese, confectioners' sugar, and orange zest until smooth.

2. In another medium bowl, beat the eggs, milk, granulated sugar, cinnamon, and vanilla.

3. Spread 2 tablespoons of the cream cheese mixture on each of 4 bread slices. Top with the remaining bread slices to form sandwiches. Press together gently.

4. Dip each French toast sandwich into the egg mixture, coating well on both sides.

5. In a large skillet, heat the oil over medium heat. Add the French toast sandwiches and cook for about 1 minute on each side, or until golden brown. Serve with warm fruit syrup.

6. For the berry syrup: In a small saucepan set over low heat, cook the syrup and berries for 2 to 4 minutes, or until the syrup takes on the color of the fruit and the fruit is warm.

7. For the orange syrup: In a small saucepan, set over low heat, combine the marmalade and syrup.

8. Add the mandarin oranges, and stir gently. Cook for 2 to 4 minutes, or until syrup turns a delicate orange color and the fruit is warm.

Sensual Scenario: You've just boarded a train that will take you from Paris through the beautiful French countryside to your final destination: the Riviera. You settle in to your luxurious cabin and close your eyes as the train begins to move. You are half-asleep when the door opens and a young steward slips inside. With a sexy French accent, he excuses himself for disturbing you and asks if he can do anything to make you more comfortable. "Surprise me," you murmur.

Menus to Make You Moan

For Your Italian Stallion

Appetizer

Gotcha Focaccia

(Pesto, Chicken, and Tomato Pizza)

Salad

Seize Her Caesar *(Caesar Salad)*

Side Dish

Que Bella Portabella

(Portabello Mushrooms with

Gorgonzola Cheese)

Main Course

Titillating Breast of Chicken

(Chicken Italiano with Broccoli

and Mushrooms)

Beverage

Fancy Licker-ish

(Licorice Liqueur with Coffee Beans)

Dessert

Tear My Suit Off *(Tiramisu)*

Peking Passion

Appetizer

Spring Roll in the Hay

(Spring Roll on a Bed of Fried Rice Noodles)

Salad

Sweet Pea Salad

(Watercress, Mandarin Orange,

and Cashew Salad)

Main Course

I'm Goo Goo Ga Ga over My Man

(Moo Goo Gai Pan)

Steamed Rice

Beverage

Woo Woo

(Cranberry Cocktail)

Dessert

Frozen Suckers

(Raspberry Frozen Popsicles)

Spicy Siesta

Appetizers

Topless Tapas

(Ham and Potato Croquettes)

Put Out the Fire Man!

(Spicy Fresh Salsa)

Side Dish

Kiss My Kabobs

(Corn and Pepper Shish Kabobs)

Main Course

Hot-to-Trot-A Enchilada

(Cheese and Onion Enchiladas)

Beverage

Hot Tomato

(Bloody Mary Cocktail)

Dessert

"Yes, You Can" Flan

(Flan with Slivered Almonds)

Luau Lei

Appetizer

Harem Hummus

(Hummus Dip)

Go Man-Go Salsa

(Mango Peach Salsa)

Salad

Cucumber Heaven

(Cucumber, Tomato, and Feta Cheese Salad)

Main Course

Chick on a Stick

(Tropical Chicken Kabobs)

Beverage

Tropical Heat

(Pineapple Rum Cocktail)

Dessert

Tarzan's Chocolate-dipped Banana with Nuts

(Frozen Chocolate-dipped Banana with Nuts)

Star Spangled Supper

Appetizer

Adam and Edam in the Garden of Eatin'

(Edam Cheese with Apple Wedges

for Dipping)

Side Dish

They Won't Make You Go Blind Carrots

(Baby Carrots with Brown Sugar)

Stuffed Studly Spuds (Twice Baked Potatoes)

Main Course

Love Me Tender

(Pork Tenderloin Roast

with Cherry-Rosemary Sauce)

Beverage

Red Wine

Dessert

Shameless Tart

(*Apple Pear Tart*)

Romance à la France

Appetizer

Honeymoon Salmon Tartare

(*Salmon Tartare*)

Side Dish

Ménage à Trois

(*Vegetable Medley*)

Main Course

Beefcake

(*Peppery Creamy Filet Mignon*)

Beverage

French Kiss

(*Champagne Cocktail*)

Dessert

Puh-lease Officer, Give Me More

(*Chocolate Mousse with Raspberry Sauce*)

The Sure-Thing Seduction

Appetizers

Gigolo Shrimp Cocktail

(*Bacon-wrapped Shrimp with
Jalapeño Jelly Dipping Sauce and
Creamy Mustard Dipping Sauce*)

Side Dish

Spear Me Asparagus

(*Asparagus Wrapped in Prosciutto*)

I'm Just Mad About Saffron Potatoes

(*Saffron Potatoes*)

Main Course

Juicy Tails (*Lobster Tails*)

Beverage

French Kiss (*Champagne Cocktail*)

Dessert

Icy Seduction (*Champagne Freeze*)

Valentine's Day Dinner

Appetizer

Oysters Rock-Yer-Fella

(*Oysters Rockefeller*)

Salad

Don't Be Blue, "I Love You" Salad

*(Blueberry, Blue Cheese, and Pecan Salad
with Raspberry Dressing)*

Side Dish

Hole-in-One Harry

*(Brussels Sprouts, Pearl Onions,
and Cherry Tomatoes)*

Main Course

Chick on a Bed of Roses

(Chicken Breast with Rose Petal Mole)

Beverage

Rosé Wine

Dessert

Luscious Lips

(Lip-shaped Raspberry Cream Tart)

The Wild Thing Spread

Appetizers

Baby Cakes

(Crab Cakes with Lemon Mustard Sauce)

Salad

South of Her Border if You Think
You Can Afford Her

(Spinach, Bacon, and Artichoke Salad)

Main Course

Between the Sheets

(Pasta and Polenta Beds with Red Pepper Sauce)

Beverage

White Wine

Dessert

Strawberries Moan-an-off

(Strawberries Romanoff)

Breakfast in Bed

Main Course

Surprise Me Frenchy Toast

(Stuffed French Toast with Fruit Syrup)

Beverages

Main Squeeze

(Screwdrivers)

Mucho Malo Mocha Java

(Chocolate Coffee)

Index

A

Almonds, Slivered, with Flan, 101–102
Aphrodisiac foods, 13
Appetizers
  Crab Cakes with Lemon Mustard
    Sauce, 23–24
  Croquettes, Ham and Potato, 21–22
  Oysters Rockefeller, 18–19
  Pizza, Pesto, Chicken, and
    Tomato, 25
  Shrimp, Bacon–wrapped,
    with Jalapeño Jelly Dipping Sauce
    and Creamy Mustard Dipping
    Sauce, 28–29
  Spring Roll on a Bed of Fried Rice
    Noodles, 19–20
  See also Dips and Spreads; Salsa
Apple
  Tart, Pear, 90–91
  Wedges for Dipping,
    Edam Cheese with, 22–23
Artichoke
  Dip, Hot, 28
  Spinach, and Bacon Salad, 38
Asparagus Wrapped in Prosciutto, 48
Avocado and Crab Salad
    with Exotic Fruit, 40

B

Baby Carrots with Brown Sugar, 47
Bacon
  Quiche, and Spinach, 111
  Shrimp, -wrapped, with Jalapeño
    Jelly Dipping Sauce and Creamy
    Mustard Dipping Sauce, 28–29
  Spinach, and Artichoke Salad, 38
Banana(s)
  Body Paints, Edible, 94–95

Chocolate-dipped, on a Stick, 93
Foster, 91
Fritters, Honey-drizzled, Served
  over Ice Cream, 99
Smoothie, Chocolate-Chip Frozen,
  81
Smoothie, Strawberry, Blueberry,
  Mango and, 79
Beef
  Filet Mignon, Peppery Creamy, 61
  Taco, 60
Berry(ies)
  erotic eating of, 12
  Frozen Juice Treats, 100–101
  Syrup, 114–115
  See also specific berries
Beverages
  Bloody Mary, 78–79
  Champagne Cocktail, 82
  Coffee, Chocolate, 80
  Cranberry Peach Cocktail, 80
  Float, Cherry Coke and Brandy,
    81–82
  Licorice Liqueur with Coffee Beans,
    82
  Pineapple-Rum Cocktail, 78
  Screwdriver, 83
  Sloe Gin Fizz, 83
  Smoothie, Chocolate-Chip Banana
    Frozen, 81
  Smoothie, Strawberry, Blueberry,
    Mango, and Banana, 79
  Bloody Mary, 78–79
Blueberry
  Blue Cheese, and Pecan Salad with
    Raspberry Dressing, 36–37
  Strawberry, Mango, and Banana
    Smoothie, 79
Blue Cheese, Blueberry, and Pecan Salad
  with Raspberry Dressing, 36–37

Body Paints, Edible, 94–95
Brandy and Cherry Coke Float, 81–82
Broccoli, Chicken, Italiano with
  Mushrooms and, 69
Brussels Sprouts, Pearl Onions, and
  Cherry Tomatoes, 50–51
Buns, Sticky, Cinnamon, 112

C

Caesar Salad, 36
Cake, Pumpkin Coffee, 113–114
Carrots, Baby, with Brown Sugar, 47
Cashew, Watercress, and Mandarin
  Orange Salad, 37–38
Champagne
  Cocktail, 82
  Freeze, 97–98
Cheese
  Blue, Blueberry, and Pecan Salad with
    Raspberry Dressing, 36–37
  Edam, with Apple Wedges for
    Dipping, 22–23
  Enchiladas, and Onion, 71–72
  Feta, Cucumber,
    and Tomato Salad, 39
  Fettuccine Alfredo, 49
  Gorgonzola, with Portabello
    Mushrooms, 46–47
  Pizza, Pesto, Chicken,
    and Tomato, 25
  Potatoes, Twice Baked, 49–50
  Tiramisu, 102–103
Cherry
  Sauce, -Rosemary, with Pork
    Tenderloin Roast, 67–68
  Turnover, Hot, 113
Cherry Coke and Brandy Float, 81–82
Cherry Tomatoes, Brussels Sprouts, and
  Pearl Onions, 50–51

Chicken
    Breast with Rose Petal Mole, 63–64
    Italiano with Broccoli and
        Mushrooms, 69
    Kabobs, Tropical, 70–71
    Moo Goo Gai Pan, 59
    Pizza, Pesto, Tomato and, 25
Chocolate
    Banana on a Stick, -dipped, 93
    Body Paints, Edible, 94–95
    Coffee, 80
    Mousse with Raspberry Sauce, 92–93
    White and Dark, Fruit and Snacks,
        -dipped, 104
Chocolate-Chip Banana Frozen
        Smoothie, 81
Cinnamon Sticky Buns, 112
Cocktail(s)
    Champagne, 82
    Cranberry Peach, 80
    Pineapple-Rum, 78
Coffee
    Beans, Licorice Liqueur with, 82
    Chocolate, 80
Coffee Cake, Pumpkin, 113–114
Corn and Pepper Shish Kabobs, 51–52
Crab
    and Avocado Salad with
        Exotic Fruit, 40
    Cakes with Lemon Mustard Sauce,
        23–24
Cranberry Peach Cocktail, 80
Croquettes, Ham and Potato, 21–22
Cucumber
    Honeydew, and Kiwi Salsa, 30–31
    Tomato, and Feta Cheese Salad, 39

D

Daiquiri, Frozen, 79
Desserts
    Banana Fritters, Honey-drizzled,
        Served over Ice Cream, 99
    Bananas Foster, 91
    Berry Frozen Juice Treats, 100–101
    Body Paints, Edible, 94–95

Champagne Freeze, 97–98
Chocolate Mousse with Raspberry
        Sauce, 92–93
Flan with Slivered Almonds,
        101–102
Fruit and Snacks, Chocolate, White
        and Dark, -dipped, 104
Sorbet, Peach, 100
Strawberries, Peppered,
        on Ice Cream, 98
Strawberries Romanoff, 103
Tart, Apple Pear, 90–91
Tart, Raspberry Cream,
        Lip-shaped, 96–97
Tiramisu, 102–103
Dipping Sauce, Jalapeño Jelly and
        Creamy Mustard, Bacon-wrapped
        Shrimp with, 28–29
Dips and Spreads
    Artichoke, Hot, 28
    Edam Cheese with Apple Wedges
        for Dipping, 22–23
    Hummus, 26

E

Edam Cheese with Apple Wedges
        for Dipping, 22–23
Edible Body Paints, 94–95
Eggs
    Benedict, 110
    French Toast, Stuffed,
        with Fruit Syrup, 114–115
    Quiche, Bacon and Spinach, 111
Enchiladas, Cheese and Onion, 71–72
Erotic eating, art of, 12

F

Feta Cheese, Cucumber,
        and Tomato Salad, 39
Fettuccine Alfredo, 49
Filet Mignon, Peppery Creamy, 61
Fish
    Salmon Tartare, 27
    with Sweet Heat, 62

See also Shellfish
Flan with Slivered Almonds, 101–102
Float, Cherry Coke and Brandy, 81–82
Foods
    aphrodisiac, 13
    erotic eating of, 12
French Toast, Stuffed, with Fruit Syrup,
        114–115
Fritters, Banana, Honey-drizzled, Served
        over Ice Cream, 99
Frozen Daiquiri, 79
Fruit
    Chocolate-dipped, White and Dark,
        104
    erotic eating of, 12
    Exotic, Crab, and Avocado Salad
        with, 40
    Syrup, French Toast, Stuffed,
        with, 114–115
    See also Berry(ies); *specific fruit*

G

Garbanzo Beans, Hummus Dip, 26
Gorgonzola Cheese, with Portabella
        Mushrooms, 46–47

H

Ham and Potato Croquettes, 21–22
Hollandaise Sauce, 110
Honeydew, Cucumber,
        and Kiwi Salsa, 30–31
Honey-drizzled Banana Fritters,
        Served over Ice Cream, 99
Hot Artichoke Dip, 28
Hot Cherry Turnover, 113
Hummus Dip, 26

I

Ice Cream
    Banana Fritters, Honey-drizzled,
        Served over, 99
    Float, Cherry Coke and Brandy,
        81–82

Smoothie, Chocolate-Chip Banana
Frozen, 81
Strawberries, Peppered, on, 98

J

Jalapeño Jelly Dipping Sauce,
Bacon-wrapped Shrimp with,
28–29

K

Kabobs
Chicken, Tropical, 70–71
Corn and Pepper, 51–52
Kiwi, Honeydew, and Cucumber Salsa,
30–31

L

Lemon Mustard Sauce with Crab Cakes,
23–24
Licorice Liqueur with Coffee Beans, 82
Lip-shaped Raspberry Cream Tart,
96–97
Liqueur, Licorice,
with Coffee Beans, 82
Lobster Tails, 72–73

M

Mandarin Orange, Watercress, and
Cashew Salad, 37–38
Mango
Salsa, Peach, 31
Smoothie, Strawberry, Blueberry,
Banana and, 79
Milk Laced with Rum, 84
Mole, Rose Petal, Chicken Breast with,
63–64
Moo Goo Gai Pan, 59
Mousse, Chocolate, with Raspberry
Sauce, 92–93
Mushroom(s)
Chicken, Italiano with Broccoli
and, 69

Portabello, with Gorgonzola Cheese,
46–47
Mussels, Scallops, and Shrimp
with Tomatoes, 66–67
Mustard
Dipping Sauce, Creamy,
with Bacon-wrapped Shrimp,
28–29
Lemon Sauce, with Crab Cakes,
23–24

N

Noodles
Pork Lo Mein, 58
Rice, Fried, Spring Roll on a Bed
of, 19–20

O

Onion(s)
and Cheese Enchiladas,
71–72
Pearl, Brussels Sprouts, and Cherry
Tomatoes, 50–51
Orange
Mandarin, Watercress, and Cashew
Salad, 37–38
Syrup, 114–115
Oysters Rockefeller, 18–19

P

Pasta
Fettuccine Alfredo, 49
and Polenta Beds with Red Pepper
Sauce, 64–66
Peach
Cocktail, Cranberry, 80
Salsa, Mango, 31
Sorbet, 100
Pear Apple Tart, 90–91
Pecan, Blueberry, and Blue Cheese Salad
with Raspberry Dressing, 36–37
Pepper(s)
and Corn Shish Kabobs, 51–52

Jalapeño Jelly Dipping Sauce,
Bacon-wrapped Shrimp with,
28–29
Red Pepper Sauce, with Pasta and
Polenta Beds, 64–66
Peppered Strawberries on Ice Cream, 98
Peppery Creamy Filet Mignon, 61
Pesto, Chicken, and Tomato Pizza, 25
Pineapple-Rum Cocktail, 78
Pizza, Pesto, Chicken, and Tomato, 25
Polenta and Pasta Beds
with Red Pepper Sauce, 64–66
Pork
Ham and Potato Croquettes, 21–22
Lo Mein, 58
Spring Roll on a Bed of Fried Rice
Noodles, 19–20
Tenderloin Roast with
Cherry-Rosemary Sauce, 67–68
See also Bacon
Portabello Mushrooms
with Gorgonzola Cheese, 46–47
Potato(es)
and Ham Croquettes, 21–22
Saffron, 52
Twice Baked, 49–50
Prosciutto, Asparagus Wrapped in, 48
Puddings, Body Paints, Edible, 94–95
Pumpkin Coffee Cake, 113–114

Q

Quiche, Bacon and Spinach, 111

R

Raspberry
Dressing, with Blueberry, Blue
Cheese, and Pecan Salad, 36–37
Sauce, with Chocolate Mousse,
92–93
Tart, Cream, Lip-shaped, 96–97
Red Pepper Sauce, with Pasta and
Polenta Beds, 64–66
Rose Petal Mole, with Chicken Breast,
63–64

Rum
    Daiquiri, Frozen, 79
    Milk Laced with, 84
    -Pineapple Cocktail, 78

S

Saffron Potatoes, 52
Salad(s)
    Blueberry, Blue Cheese, and Pecan,
        with Raspberry Dressing, 36–37
    Caesar, 36
    Crab and Avocado, with Exotic Fruit,
        40
    Cucumber, Tomato, and Feta Cheese,
        39
    Spinach, Bacon, and Artichoke, 38
    Watercress, Mandarin Orange, and
        Cashew, 37–38
Salmon Tartare, 27
Salsa
    Honeydew, Cucumber, and Kiwi,
        30–31
    Mango Peach, 31
    Spicy Fresh, 24–25
Sauce(s)
    Cherry-Rosemary, with Pork
        Tenderloin Roast, 67–68
    Dipping, Jalapeño Jelly and Creamy
        Mustard, with Bacon-wrapped
        Shrimp, 28–29
    Hollandaise, 110
    Lemon Mustard, with Crab Cakes,
        23–24
    Raspberry, with Chocolate Mousse,
        92
    Red Pepper, with Pasta and Polenta
        Beds, 64–66
Scallops, Mussels, and Shrimp with
    Tomatoes, 66–67
Screwdriver, 83
Shellfish
    Crab and Avocado Salad, with Exotic
        Fruit, 40
    Crab Cakes with Lemon Mustard
        Sauce, 23–24

Lobster Tails, 72–73
Mussels, Scallops, and Shrimp
    with Tomatoes, 66–67
Oysters Rockefeller, 18–19
Shrimp, Bacon-wrapped, with
    Jalapeño Jelly Dipping Sauce and
    Creamy Mustard Dipping Sauce,
    28–29
Shish Kabobs, Corn and Pepper, 51–52
Shrimp
    Bacon-wrapped, with Jalapeño Jelly
        Dipping Sauce and Creamy Mustard
        Dipping Sauce, 28–29
    Mussels, and Scallops with Tomatoes,
        66–67
Sloe Gin Fizz, 83
Smoothie
    Chocolate-Chip Banana Frozen, 81
    Strawberry, Blueberry, Mango, and
        Banana, 79
Snacks, Chocolate-dipped, White
    and Dark, 104
Sorbet, Peach, 100
Spicy Salsa, Fresh, 24–25
Spinach
    Bacon, and Artichoke Salad, 38
    Quiche, and Bacon, 111
Spring Roll on a Bed of Fried Rice
    Noodles, 19–20
Steak, Filet Mignon, Peppery Creamy,
    61
Sticky Buns, Cinnamon, 112
Strawberry(ies)
    Body Paints, Edible, 94–95
    Peppered, on Ice Cream, 98
    Romanoff, 103
    Smoothie, Blueberry, Mango, Banana
        and, 79
Stuffed French Toast with Fruit Syrup,
    114–115
Syrup, Fruit, French Toast, Stuffed,
    with, 114–115

T

Taco, Beef, 60

Tart(s)
    Apple Pear, 90–91
    Raspberry Cream, Lip-shaped, 96–97
Tiramisu, 102–103
Tomato(es)
    Cherry, Brussels Sprouts, and Pearl
        Onions, 50–51
    Cucumber, and Feta Cheese Salad, 39
    Mussels, Scallops, and Shrimp with,
        66–67
    Pizza, Pesto, Chicken and, 25
    Salsa, Spicy Fresh, 24–25
Tortillas
    Enchiladas, Cheese and Onion,
        71–72
    Taco, Beef, 60
Tropical Chicken Kabobs, 70–71
Turnover, Hot Cherry, 113
Twice Baked Potatoes, 49–50

V

Vegetable(s)
    Medley, 46
    See also specific vegetables
Vodka
    Bloody Mary, 78–79
    Cranberry Peach Cocktail, 80
    Screwdriver, 83

W

Watercress, Mandarin Orange, and
    Cashew Salad, 37–38
White and Dark Chocolate-dipped Fruit
    and Snacks, 104

For Our International Audience

Conversion Tables

Generic Formulas for Metric Conversion

ounces to grams....................multiply ounces by 28.35
pounds to grams...................multiply pounds by 453.5
cups to liters.........................multiply cups by .24
Fahrenheit to centigrade........subtract 32 from Fahrenheit, multiply by five and divide by 9

Metric Equivalents for Volume

U.S.	Imperial	Metric
⅛ tsp.	—	.6 ml.
½ tsp.	—	2.5 ml.
¾ tsp.	—	4 ml.
1 tsp.	—	5 ml.
1½ tsp.	—	7 ml.
2 tsp.	—	10 ml.
3 tsp.	—	15 ml.
4 tsp.	—	20 ml.
1 Tbsp.	—	15 ml.
1½ Tbsp.	—	22 ml.
2 Tbsp. (⅛ cup)	1 fl. oz.	30 ml.
2½ Tbsp.	—	37 ml.
3 Tbsp.	—	44 ml.
⅓ cup	—	57 ml.
4 Tbsp. (¼ cup)	2 fl. oz.	59 ml.
5 Tbsp.	—	74 ml.
6 Tbsp.	—	89 ml.
8 Tbsp. (½ cup)	3 fl. oz.	120 ml.
¾ cup	6 fl. oz.	178 ml.
1 cup	8 fl. oz.	237 ml.
1½ cups	—	354 ml.
1¾ cups	—	414 ml.
2 cups (1 pint)	—	473 ml.
5 cups	—	1183 ml. (1.183 liters)

Oven Temperatures

Degrees Fahrenheit	Degrees Centigrade	British Gas Marks
100°	37.8°	—
160°	71.1°	—
275°	140°	1
300°	150°	2
325°	165°	3
350°	175°	4
375°	190°	5
400°	200°	6
450°	230°	8

Metric Equivalents for Weight

U.S.	Metric
1 oz.	28 g.
2 oz.	58 g.
3 oz.	85 g.
4 oz. (¼ lb.)	113 g.
5 oz.	142 g.
6 oz.	170 g.
7 oz.	199 g.
8 oz. (½ lb.)	227 g.
10 oz.	284 g.
12 oz. (¾ lb.)	340 g.
14 oz.	397 g.
16 oz. (1 lb.)	454 g.
18 oz.	510 g.
20 oz. (1¼ lb.)	567 g.
25 oz.	709 g.
28 oz.	794 g.

Metric Equivalents for Butter

U.S.	Metric
2 tsp.	10 g.
1 Tbsp.	15 g.
1½ Tbsp.	22.5 g.
2 Tbsp. (1 oz.)	55 g.
3 Tbsp.	70 g.
¼ lb. (1 stick)	110 g.
½ lb. (2 sticks)	220 g.

Metric Equivalents for Length
(use also for pan sizes)

U.S.	Metric
¼ in.	¾ cm.
½ in.	1½ cm.
1 inch	3 cm.
2 in.	5 cm.
3 in.	6 cm.
4 in.	8 cm.
5 in.	11 cm.
6 in.	12 cm.
7 in.	14 cm.
8 in.	20 cm.
9 in.	23 cm.
12 in.	30 cm.
13 in.	33 cm.
14 in.	36 cm.

Cooking Terms

United States	British Equivalent/Substitute
bacon	streaky bacon
bacon, Canadian	cooked, cured gammon ham
biscuit, refrigerated	may substitute frozen/refrigerated puff or bun pastry
broil (verb)	to grill
cheese, Cheddar	may substitute any shreddable orange cheese
cheese, Monterey Jack	may substitute any shreddable white cheese
cilantro	coriander
cornstarch	cornflour
cream, heavy	double cream
cream, light	single cream
double boiler	double saucepan
desserts	puddings
filet	fillet
filet mignon	fillet of beef
flour, all-purpose	plain flour
garbanzo bean	chick-pea
green onion	spring onion
honey mustard	equal parts honey and mustard
jalapeño jelly	Jamaican hot jelly
jalapeño pepper	green chile
jicama strips	may substitute water chestnuts
kabob	kebab
ladyfinger	sponge finger
lettuce, bibb or Boston	lambs lettuce or baby cos lettuce
lettuce, romaine	cos lettuce
pie crust	pastry case
pita bread	pitta
pitted	stoned
pork tenderloin	fillet of pork roast
portabello mushroom	may substitute large, flat mushroom
prosciutto	Parma ham
pumpkin purée, canned	may substitute canned carrot
pumpkin pie spice mix	cinnamon, cloves, allspice, and mace
purée (verb)	to pulp
Queso Fresco	may substitute Wensleydale cheese
sauce, steak	may substitute with Worcestershire sauce
serrano pepper	green chile
shot	jigger
shrimp	prawn
snow pea	sugar snap pea
spatula	fish slice or palette knife
sugar, brown/light brown	demerara sugar
sugar, confectioner's	icing sugar
sugar, granulated	cane sugar
sugar, superfine	caster sugar
vanilla pudding	vanilla yogurt
whole wheat	wholemeal
yellow cake mix	vanilla cake mix
yellow squash	may substitute yellow bell pepper
zest, orange/lemon	when zest required, use unwaxed rind
zucchini	courgette

About the Chippendales®

The Chippendales® story began in 1979, when this all-male dance group performed for the first time in a Los Angeles nightclub. Named for the high quality and beautiful curves of the elegant eighteenth-century furniture designed by Thomas Chippendale, the Chippendales® soon opened their own club in Los Angeles. Ladies now had a fantasyland of their very own.

The Chippendales® honed their cabaret-style show in the 1980s, touring the United States and opening a second club in New York City. They took their act to such faraway lands as the United Kingdom, South Africa, Scandinavia, Europe, and more. Women worldwide proved susceptible to the hunky, boy-next-door dancers in G-strings who exchanged kisses for dollar bills.

The Chippendales® continued to tour the globe throughout the 1990s, expanding their show to a full-blown theater review—a two-hour montage of twenty to thirty dance routines starring a cast of sixteen. Many of the dancers have been part of major productions like *Cats* and *Starlight Express,* not to mention large-scale tours for such performers as Madonna, Whitney Houston, Gloria Estefan, and others. Despite what you may think, having a muscular body is not a prerequisite for becoming a Chippendale—the most important factors are individuality, personality, and talent as a performer.

So keep an eye out for the Chippendales® as they continue to tour into the next millennium. Who knows—they might be appearing soon at a kitchen near you.